First World War
and Army of Occupation
War Diary
France, Belgium and Germany

25 DIVISION
75 Infantry Brigade,
Brigade Machine Gun Company
19 December 1915 - 1 May 1917

WO95/2251/5

The Naval & Military Press Ltd
www.nmarchive.com
Published in association with The National Archives

Published by

The Naval & Military Press Ltd

Unit 10 Ridgewood Industrial Park,

Uckfield, East Sussex,

TN22 5QE England

Tel: +44 (0) 1825 749494

www.naval-military-press.com

www.nmarchive.com

This diary has been reprinted in facsimile from the original. Any imperfections are inevitably reproduced and the quality may fall short of modern type and cartographic standards.

© **Crown Copyright**
Images reproduced by permission of The National Archives, London, England, 2015.

Contents

Document type	Place/Title	Date From	Date To
Heading	WO95/2251-5		
Heading	75th Machine Gun Coy. Mar 1916-Feb 1918		
Heading	75th Machine Gun Company, 9th Marc to 2nd June, 1916		
Miscellaneous	75th Co V Machine Gun Corps	06/06/1916	06/06/1916
War Diary	Grantham	19/12/1915	10/03/1916
War Diary	Southampton	10/03/1916	10/03/1916
War Diary	Le Havre	11/03/1916	13/03/1916
War Diary	Abbeville	14/03/1916	14/03/1916
War Diary	St Pol	14/03/1916	14/03/1916
War Diary	Aubigny	14/03/1916	14/03/1916
War Diary	Grossart	15/03/1916	26/03/1916
War Diary	Neuville-St-Vaast	29/03/1916	29/03/1916
War Diary	Grossart	28/03/1916	29/03/1916
War Diary	Bailleul	30/03/1916	30/03/1916
War Diary	Neuville-St-Vaast	02/04/1916	02/04/1916
War Diary	Bailleul	01/04/1916	01/04/1916
War Diary	Neuvill-St-Vaast	04/04/1916	04/04/1916
War Diary	Bailleul	04/04/1916	19/04/1916
War Diary	Neuville-St-Vaast	20/04/1916	02/06/1916
Heading	75th Machine Gun Company, 7th to June, 1916.		
Miscellaneous	75 Coy Machine Gun Corps.	19/07/1916	19/07/1916
War Diary	Bethonsart	07/06/1916	13/06/1916
War Diary	Neuville-au-Cornet	14/06/1916	15/06/1916
War Diary	Bonnieres	16/06/1916	17/06/1916
War Diary	Bernaville	18/06/1916	18/06/1916
War Diary	St Ouen	19/06/1916	24/06/1916
War Diary	Talmas	25/06/1916	27/06/1916
War Diary	Toutencourt	28/06/1916	30/06/1916
Heading	75th Machine Gun Company July 1916		
War Diary		01/07/1916	27/07/1916
War Diary	Auchonvillers	27/07/1916	31/07/1916
Heading	75th Brigade Machine Gun Company August 1916		
Miscellaneous	75 Machine Gun Coy	04/09/1916	04/09/1916
War Diary	Auchonvillers	01/08/1916	09/08/1916
War Diary	St Leger-Les-Authie	10/08/1916	10/08/1916
War Diary	Authie	11/08/1916	13/08/1916
War Diary	Hedauville	20/08/1916	27/08/1916
War Diary	Authville	28/08/1916	31/08/1916
Heading	75th. Machine Gun Company September 1916		
War Diary	Authville	01/09/1916	07/09/1916
War Diary	South Bluff	08/09/1916	08/09/1916
War Diary	Lealvillers	08/09/1916	10/09/1916
War Diary	Orville	10/09/1916	11/09/1916
War Diary	Boisbergues	11/09/1916	12/09/1916
War Diary	Cramont	12/09/1916	25/09/1916
War Diary	Amplier	25/09/1916	26/09/1916
War Diary	Acheux	26/09/1916	29/09/1916
War Diary	Bouzincourt	29/09/1916	30/09/1916
Heading	75th Machine Gun Company October 1916		

Miscellaneous	75 Machine Gun Coy	02/11/1916	02/11/1916
War Diary	Pozieres	01/10/1916	06/10/1916
War Diary	Bouzincourt	07/10/1916	15/10/1916
War Diary	Pointx 2b 0.4	16/10/1916	18/10/1916
War Diary	Pointx 2b 0.4 Sheet 57d SE.	18/10/1916	21/10/1916
War Diary	X 2b 0.4.	22/10/1916	22/10/1916
War Diary	Bouzincourt	23/10/1916	23/10/1916
War Diary	Warloy	23/10/1916	24/10/1916
War Diary	Authieule	24/10/1916	30/10/1916
War Diary	Meteren	31/10/1916	31/10/1916
Heading	75th Machine Gun Company, November, 1916.		
Miscellaneous	75th Machine Gun Coy	01/12/1916	01/12/1916
War Diary	Meteren	01/11/1916	01/11/1916
War Diary	Le Romarin	01/11/1916	29/11/1916
Heading	75th Machine Gun Company, December, 1916		
War Diary	Romarin	01/12/1916	02/01/1917
War Diary	Carters Camp De Seule	03/01/1917	16/01/1917
War Diary	Le Bizet	17/01/1917	31/01/1917
Miscellaneous	75 Machine Gun Coy	01/03/1917	01/03/1917
War Diary	Le Bizet	01/02/1917	25/02/1917
War Diary	Romarin	26/02/1917	26/02/1917
War Diary	Eecke Area	27/02/1917	28/02/1917
Miscellaneous	75 Machine Gun Coy	01/04/1917	01/04/1917
War Diary	Eecke Area	01/03/1917	13/03/1917
War Diary	Wardrecques	14/03/1917	14/03/1917
War Diary	Seninghem	15/03/1917	20/03/1917
War Diary	Cormette	21/03/1917	21/03/1917
War Diary	Renescure	22/03/1917	22/03/1917
War Diary	Swartenbrouck	23/03/1917	24/03/1917
War Diary	Bleu Tour	25/03/1917	05/04/1917
War Diary	Neuve Eglise	06/04/1917	12/04/1917
War Diary	Steen-Je	13/04/1917	19/04/1917
War Diary	Le Bizet	20/04/1917	29/04/1917
War Diary	Erquinghem-Lts	30/04/1917	30/04/1917
Miscellaneous	75 Machine Gun Coy	01/05/1917	01/05/1917
War Diary	Bleu Tour	01/05/1917	10/05/1917
War Diary	Steent-Je	10/05/1917	14/05/1917
War Diary	La Creche	15/05/1917	29/05/1917
War Diary	Ravelsburg	30/05/1917	31/05/1917
Miscellaneous	75 M.G. Coy	02/07/1917	02/07/1917
War Diary	Ravelsburg	01/06/1917	05/06/1917
War Diary	T 1 C Central	06/06/1917	07/06/1917
War Diary	Sheet 28 SW O31A	07/06/1917	18/06/1917
War Diary	T 1 C Central	19/06/1917	23/06/1917
War Diary	La Motte	24/06/1917	24/06/1917
War Diary	Merville	25/06/1917	25/06/1917
War Diary	Lespesses	26/06/1917	26/06/1917
War Diary	Petigny	27/06/1917	30/06/1917
Miscellaneous	75 Machine Gun Coy	06/08/1917	06/08/1917
War Diary	Petigny	01/07/1917	08/07/1917
War Diary	Tannay	09/07/1917	09/07/1917
War Diary	Halifax Camp	10/07/1917	22/07/1917
War Diary	Lorna Camp	23/07/1917	30/07/1917
War Diary	Belgian Chateau Area	31/07/1917	31/07/1917
Miscellaneous	75 Machine Gun Coy.	31/08/1917	31/08/1917
War Diary	Beck Trench	01/08/1917	05/08/1917

War Diary	Pioneer Camp	06/08/1917	17/08/1917
War Diary	Eecke	18/08/1917	20/08/1917
War Diary	Steenvoorde	21/08/1917	22/08/1917
War Diary	Winniezeele	23/08/1917	31/08/1917
Miscellaneous	75 Machine Gun Coy	02/10/1917	02/10/1917
War Diary	Oudezeele	01/09/1917	01/09/1917
War Diary	Dickebusch	02/09/1917	05/09/1917
War Diary	Halfway House	06/09/1917	09/09/1917
War Diary	Dickebusch	10/09/1917	10/09/1917
War Diary	Halifox Camp	11/09/1917	12/09/1917
War Diary	Caestre	13/09/1917	13/09/1917
War Diary	Tannay	14/09/1917	14/09/1917
War Diary	Marles Les Mines	15/09/1917	27/09/1917
War Diary	Noeux Les Mines	28/09/1917	29/09/1917
War Diary	Cite St Pierre	30/09/1917	05/10/1917
War Diary	Noeux Les Mines	06/10/1917	06/10/1917
War Diary	Le Preol	07/10/1917	10/10/1917
War Diary	Beuvry	11/10/1917	20/10/1917
War Diary	Le Preol	21/10/1917	31/10/1917
Miscellaneous	75th Machine Gun Coy.	02/12/1917	02/12/1917
War Diary	Le Preol	01/11/1917	29/11/1917
War Diary	Burbure	30/11/1917	30/11/1917
War Diary	Petigny	30/11/1917	30/11/1917
War Diary	Petigny	01/12/1917	01/12/1917
War Diary	Vinchy	02/12/1917	03/12/1917
War Diary	Achiet Le Grand	04/12/1917	04/12/1917
War Diary	Gomiecourt	05/12/1917	05/12/1917
War Diary	Rocquigny	06/12/1917	09/12/1917
War Diary	Bapaume	10/12/1917	11/12/1917
War Diary	Favreul	12/12/1917	21/12/1917
War Diary	Lagnicourt	22/12/1917	02/01/1918
War Diary	Favreul	03/01/1918	13/01/1918
War Diary	Favreul	20/01/1918	26/01/1918
War Diary	Lagnicourt	27/01/1918	31/01/1918
Miscellaneous	C Coy 25 Battalion M.G.C.	01/03/1918	01/03/1918
War Diary	Lagnicourt	01/02/1918	11/02/1918
War Diary	Favreul	12/02/1918	12/02/1918
War Diary	Buchanan Camp Achiet Le Petit	13/02/1918	28/02/1918
War Diary	75 Machine Gun Coy	01/05/1917	01/05/1917

No 95/2251/5

25TH DIVISION
75TH INFY BDE

75TH MACHINE GUN COY.
MAR 1916 - FEB 1918

25TH DIVISION
75TH INFY BDE

75th Inf. Bde.

25th Division

75th MACHINE GUN COMPANY,

9TH MARCH to 2nd JUNE, 1 9 1 6.

(Company disembarked Harve 11.3.16 from U.K.)

MGC 395

From O.C.
  75 Co^y Machine Gun Corps.

To D.A.G
  3rd Echelon.

         June 6-16.
 Herewith please find War diary completed to end of May.
 I regret the delay in forwarding this but owing to the strenuous labours attached to our duty in the trenches the compilation of the Diary was somewhat interfered with.
 In future there will be no delay

      R Cochrane   Captain.
    Commanding 75 Co^y
     MACHINE GUN CORPS.

75 M.G. Coy
Vol I
25

Army Form C. 2118.

WAR DIARY
or
INTELLIGENCE SUMMARY

(Erase heading not required.)

Instructions regarding War Diaries and Intelligence Summaries are contained in F. S. Regs., Part II. and the Staff Manual respectively. Title Pages will be prepared in manuscript.

Place	Date	Hour	Summary of Events and Information	Remarks and references to Appendices
GRANTHAM	19/12/15		Formation of 75th MG Coy. & posting of officers	
GRANTHAM			Training of men commenced.	
GRANTHAM			Mobilization commenced	
GRANTHAM	9/3/16	9.30 pm	The unit left GRANTHAM CAMP	
GRANTHAM	10/3/16	12.45 am	Entrained at GRANTHAM station	
SOUTHAMPTON	10/3/16	11.30 am	Arrived at SOUTHAMPTON	
SOUTHAMPTON	10/3/16	8 pm	Sailed from SOUTHAMPTON. Unit proceeded in two vessels. One for Rouen river, one for transport	
LE HAVRE	11/3/16	5 am	Arrived at LE HAVRE & proceeded to "Rest Camp"	
"	"	11 am	Arrived at "Rest Camp"	
"	13/3/16	5 pm	Completion of RestCamp routine consisting of Parades & Inspections & departure for LE HAVRE station	
"	"	10 pm	Entrained at LE HAVRE station	
ABBEVILLE	14/3/16	2 am	Halt at ABBEVILLE for hot coffee	
ST POL	"	2 pm	Halt at ST POL	
AUBIGNY	"	5 pm	Arrived at AUBIGNY.	
"	"	7.15 pm	Departure from AUBIGNY.	

WAR DIARY
or
INTELLIGENCE SUMMARY
(Erase heading not required.)

Army Form C. 2118.

Place	Date	Hour	Summary of Events and Information	Remarks and references to Appendices
GROSSART	15/3/16	2 a.m.	Arrived at GROSSART & proceeded to Billets previously selected by Brigade.	
"	16/3/16		Work of Company revised & further training with Civilians commenced.	
"	28/3/16	4.30 pm	No 1 Section leaves GROSSART for 48 hrs instruction in trenches at NEUVILLE-ST-VAAST.	
NEUVILLE-ST-VAAST	29/3/16	2.30 pm	Heavy shelling by the Enemy preparatory to the blowing up of a mine in the evening. One casualty — Pte ARCHARD killed.	
GROSSART	29/3/16	1 pm	No 3 Section leaves GROSSART to relief No 1 Sec. Billets the night at Savy. Proceeds the next day to ECOIVRE, where it was given orders to proceed at once to NEUVILLE-ST-VAAST. Owing to the fact of its still being daylight the section was held up at the Artillery (18 phr) trenches till 9.30 pm, after which it was safe to continue. The section then proceeded to NEUVILLE-ST-VAAST relieving No 1 Sec.	
GROSSART	29/3/16		The remainder of the Company proceeded to new billets in BAILLEUL-AUX-CORNAILLES	
BAILLEUL	30/3/16	2 pm	No 2 Sec. leaves BAILLEUL to relieve No 3 Sec, billets at Savy, & proceeds the following day to ECOIVRE & then on to NEUVILLE-ST-VAAST in the evening.	

Army Form C. 2118.

WAR DIARY
or
INTELLIGENCE SUMMARY
(Erase heading not required.)

Instructions regarding War Diaries and Intelligence Summaries are contained in F. S. Regs, Part II. and the Staff Manual respectively. Title Pages will be prepared in manuscript.

Place	Date	Hour	Summary of Events and Information	Remarks and references to Appendices
NEUVILLE-St-VAAST	2/4/16	5 pm	where it relieved No 3 Section.	
			The Enemy Sprang a mine & outposted our lines to a severe bombardment.	
BAILLEUL	3/4/16	2 pm	No 4 Sec. leaves BAILLEUL to relieve No 2 Sec. & billets the night at Savy & proceeds the next day to ECOIVRES & then on to NEUVILLE-St-VAAST, where it relieved No 2 Sec.	
NEUVILLE-St-VAAST	4/4/16	9 pm	No 4 Sec leaves the trenches & proceeds to Savy where it billeted the night & then proceeded on to BAILLEUL.	
BAILLEUL	7/4/16		LT LOVE posted to the Company as 2nd in Command.	
	8/4/16		The Coy took part in a Brigade Scheme of attacking at night an enemy holding line between BAILLEUL FARM & the village of CHELERS. Sections of the 73rd MG Coy were attached to the battalions of the 75th Brigade. Their particular task was to advance with & protect the flanks of their respective battalions. This was carried out successfully.	
"	14/4/16		March past & inspection by the Corps Commander.	
"	10/4/16		Tactical scheme arranged by Capt R Cochrane, & approved by the Brigadier	

Army Form C. 2118.

75 Bn M.G Coy (75 Div)
19/4 – 2/6/16

WAR DIARY

Instructions regarding War Diaries and Intelligence Summaries are contained in F. S. Regs., Part II. and the Staff Manual respectively. Title Pages will be prepared in manuscript.

(Erase heading not required.)

Place	Date	Hour	Summary of Events and Information	Remarks and references to Appendices
BAILLEUL	19/4/16	2 pm	The whole Company moved to ECOIVRES.	
NEUVILLE-ST-VAAST	20/4/16	9 pm	The Coy relieved the 137 MG Coy at NEUVILLE-ST-VAAST. No 3 Section took over emplacements 2,3,4,5,6. No 4 Section, emplacements 3,7,8,9. No 2 Section took over the NEUVILLE emplacements – Nos 11,12,13,14,15 & 16. No 1 Sec remained at ECOIVRES.	
"	25/4/16		Sectional relief. It was found to be necessary to have a different system of relief for Officers relieving, as there were not sufficient Officers to remain with their Sections throughout the different reliefs. No 3 Sec took over emplacements 12,13,14,15,16. No 2 Sec took over Nos 7,8,9. No 1 Sec Nos 2,3,4. No 4 Sec proceeded to ECOIVRES	
"	26/4/16	9 pm	Overhead fire was carried out from No 16 position on the village of THÉLUS, with the object of catching enemy transport	
"	30/4/16		Sectional relief. No 4 Sec to Left Sector (emps 7,8,9), No 3 to Right Sector (emps 2,3,4,5,6). No 2 to NEUVILLE, No 2 to ECOIVRES.	
"	2/4/16	10 pm	Overhead fire from No 15 position on hostile communication trenches.	

WAR DIARY or INTELLIGENCE SUMMARY

Army Form C. 2118.

Place	Date	Hour	Summary of Events and Information	Remarks and references to Appendices
NEUVILLE-ST-VAAST	5/5/16		Sectional relief. No 1 Sec to Right Sector, No 2 to Left, No 3 & Ecoivres, No 4 to NEUVILLE.	
"		2.30 pm	The enemy sprung a mine and blew up a listening post on the right of our No 4 position. Captain R Cochrane arrived at No 1 before the gun, but in the excitement the iron plate was not removed & this resulted in Capt R Cochrane receiving a slight wound from a ricochet bullet. Overhead fire carried out from No 1 S position on THELUS & from No 11 position on THELUS	
"	6/5/16			
"	10/5/16		Sectional relief No 1 to Right Sector, No 3 Left Sector, No 2 to NEUVILLE. No 4 to Right Sector, No 4 to Ecoivres.	
"	12/5/16	3 pm	Machine Guns in conjunction with Artillery, Trench Mortars, fired on enemy trenches. Trench mortars & artillery fired on enemy front line in front of our left sector. MGs from positions 15,16 +11 fired on the enemy's communication trenches behind this point. One gun from No 11 position fired on THELUS.	
"	13/5/16	9 pm	Overhead fire on enemy communication trenches from No 15 position & on	

Army Form C. 2118.

WAR DIARY
or
INTELLIGENCE SUMMARY
(Erase heading not required.)

Instructions regarding War Diaries and Intelligence Summaries are contained in F. S. Regs., Part II and the Staff Manual respectively. Title Pages will be prepared in manuscript.

Place	Date	Hour	Summary of Events and Information	Remarks and references to Appendices
NEUVILLE-ST VAAST	14/5/16	9.30pm	THÉLUS. Enemy MG retaliated.	
"	15/5/16		Work of 15/5/16. retaliated. Sectorial relief. No 1 to Right Sectr, No 2 to ECOIVRES. No 3 to NEUVILLE & No 4 to Reserve Left Sector.	
"	17/5/16		Overhead fire from No 15 Position on enemy communication trenches. Enemy M.G. retaliated. The NEUVILLE-ST-VAAST road was swept at regular intervals by enemy fire. No casualties.	
"	19/5/16		Overhead fire from No 11 Position on THÉLUS	
"	20/5/16		Sectorial relief. No 4 to Left Sectr, No 3 Right Sectr, No 2 to NEUVILLE & No 1 to ECOIVRES	
"	21/5/16		Owing to a shell unexpectedly falling & exploding in NEUVILLE 2nd Lieut & Pte LYALL were slightly wounded.	
"	22/5/16	10pm	Overhead fire from No 15 Position on enemy communication trenches & from No 11 point on THÉLUS. Enemy gun retaliated.	
"	23/5/16	4.1am	MGs from positions 15&16 took part in the attack by the 74th Brigade.	

WAR DIARY
or
INTELLIGENCE SUMMARY

Army Form C. 2118.

Place	Date	Hour	Summary of Events and Information	Remarks and references to Appendices
NEUVILLE-St-VAAST	24/5/16	4 p.m.	Their guns fired on enemy communication trenches behind the front of attack. The enemy's bombardment extended down left sector, where their guns were situated. Position T & F suffered considerably, the latter being practically demolished. Cpl Harrod was wounded somewhat severely through left thigh by shrapnel. Overhead fire from No 15 position over saw trenches as were fires on left westerly of trenches. Also from No 11 position on THELUS. At this position Pt SABINE was unfortunately wounded by our own fire, owing to a live cartridge being by accident left in the barrel of the gun.	
"	25/5/16		Sectional relief. No 1 to Right sector, No 2 to Left Sector, No 3 to ECOIVRES, No 4 to NEUVILLE.	
"	26/5/16		Overhead fire from No 15 posn on THELUS, also from No 11 position.	
"	27/5/16		Machine Guns co-operated with artillery & trench mortars in firing on enemy trenches in front of our Right Sector. Our artillery & trench	

Army Form C. 2118.

WAR DIARY
or
INTELLIGENCE SUMMARY
(Erase heading not required.)

Instructions regarding War Diaries and Intelligence Summaries are contained in F. S. Regs., Part II. and the Staff Manual respectively. Title Pages will be prepared in manuscript.

Place	Date	Hour	Summary of Events and Information	Remarks and references to Appendices
NEUVILLE-ST VAAST	2/4/16		Mortars fired on enemy front-line, while M.G. from position 11.15 swept the communication trenches behind this front. Our Company relieved from trenches. The 153 Brigade took over the Right Sector. The M.G. Coy of this Brigade placed Vickers guns only in 2 of our positions, Nos 2 & 3. The Brigade took over our own Left Sector. The M.G. Coy of this Brigade placed only 2 guns in this center — positions 7 & 9. The 75th Coy M.G. Corps then proceeded with all equipment to ECOIVRES. On the evening of thursday, the Coy proceeded to billets in the village of BETHONSART.	

75th Inf. Bde.

25th Division

75th MACHINE GUN COMPANY.

7th to 30th J U N E, 1 9 1 6.

OM 196.

From O.C.
    75 Coy. Machine Gun Corps.

To D.A.G.
    3rd Echelon

19-7-16

Herewith please find War diary, (original) for month ended 30-6-16.
I reg't delay in submitting this due to the Coy being engaged on active operations.

_____ Captain,
Commanding 75 Coy
    MACHINE GUN CORPS

75 M.G. Coy
Vol 2
XXV

WAR DIARY
~~INTELLIGENCE~~ SUMMARY
(Erase heading not required.)

Place	Date	Hour	Summary of Events and Information	Remarks and references to Appendices
BETHONSART	7.6.16	6 a.m.	Company engaged on scheme — Attacking Tactical point. Returned to Billets 4 p.m.	
"	8.6.16	11:30 a.m.	Each Section of Company now attached to each Battalion in Brigade who carried out schemes of attack.	
"	9.6.16	8 a.m.	Company marched to MONCHY-BRETON arriving 10:30 a.m. & then incorporated in Brigade scheme.	
"	"	3 p.m.	The Company was inspected by General Gumal. Company arrived at Billets 8 p.m.	
"	10.6.16	7 a.m.	Whole Company taken to Divisional Baths at TINQUES.	
"	11.6.16	6 a.m.	Brigade Exercise at HERLIN-LE-VERT. Sections cooperated with Battalions. Sgt. Graham obtained time.	
"	12.6.16	5 a.m.	Company carried out M.G. Training in morning. Company tested its first Mule, leg broken by a	
"	"		kick. Start by Veterinary N.C.O. during Company noted in afternoon.	
"	13.6.16	4:30 a.m.	Divisional manoeuvres. Company march to La THIEULOYE — carry out junction orders.	
"	"		Scheme: Attack on MERLIN-LE-VERT. Returned to Billets 6 p.m. Instructions to move.	
BETHONSART NEUVILLE-AU-CORNET	14.6.16	10 a.m.	Company left BETHONSART. Arrived at NEUVILLE AU CORNET 2:30 p.m.	
NEUVILLE-AU-CORNET	15.6.16	8 a.m.	The Company left NEUVILLE AU CORNET. Arrived BONNIERES 11:30 a.m.	
BONNIERES	16.6.16	6 a.m.	Sections entrained. Afternoon carried out M.G. Training.	
BONNIERES	17.6.16	6 a.m.	General routine in morning. Left BONNIERES at 11:30 p.m.	
BERNAVILLE	18.6.16	3:45 a.m.	Arrived at BERNAVILLE 3:45 a.m. Departed 12 midnight.	
St OUEN	19.6.16	3 a.m.	Company arrived at St OUEN 3 a.m. Company Pmd Cook attained from TOUTENCOURT.	

Army Form C. 2118.

WAR DIARY
or
INTELLIGENCE SUMMARY.
(Erase heading not required.)

Instructions regarding War Diaries and Intelligence Summaries are contained in F. S. Regs., Part II. and the Staff Manual respectively. Title pages will be prepared in manuscript.

Place	Date	Hour	Summary of Events and Information	Remarks and references to Appendices
ST OUEN	20.6.16	8 am	Company allotted area for training. Training from 8 am until 1 p.m. Bath at Rubibis 2 pm.	
"	21.6.16	6 am	Breakfast made by Company in morning. Training in Training Area 1 pm - 4 pm. 1st hour 2nd in Command reums notes returned to England report to M.G. HQ 2nd Grantham	
"	22.6.16	8 am	Company in training area 8 am - 1 pm. 1st hour dispatch 10.30 am. Brigade Cross Country race	
"		9.45 pm	Company into 38 min. Captain Cochrane returned from leave. Arrived 12.15 pm.	
"	23.6.16	8 am	Company practice attack in training area	
"	24.6.16	8 am	Company inspected by Divisional General & Brigadier General whilst carrying out practice & attached under cover. Returned to Billets 12.30 pm. Instructions to move. Left ST OUEN 11 pm.	
TALMAS	25.6.16	3.30 am	Arrived TALMAS. Company afterwards settling in Billets noted	
"	26.6.16		Company carried out M.G. Training.	
"	27.6.16		Company in Training. Instructions to move. Left Talmas 10 p.m.	
TOUTENCOURT	28.6.16	1 am	Company arrived at TOUTENCOURT and settled in Billets during day	
"	29.6.16		Company refitted, afterwards carried out training.	
"	30.6.16		Company received in morning. Instructions to move. Left TOUTENCOURT 10 p.m.	

75th Bde.
25th Div.

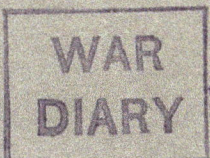

75th MACHINE GUN COMPANY

JULY 1916

Instructions regarding. War Diaries and Intelligence Summaries are contained in F. S. Regs., Part II and the Staff Manual respectively. Title Pages will be prepared in manuscript.

INTELLIGENCE SUMMARY

(Erase heading not required.)

Vol 3

Place	Date	Hour	Summary of Events and Information	Remarks and references to Appendices
	1-7-16	2 AM	Arrived HEDAUVILLE.	
	1-7-16		Orders were received to be prepared to move into action immediately on receipt of further orders.	
	2-7-16		Received orders to proceed to E. end of MARTINSART WOOD and to move via ENGLEBELMER. Orders carried out. Arrived destination about 7.0 p.m. At 10 p.m. Company was ordered to prepare to attack Enemy trenches S. of THIEPVAL. Attack timed to take place at 3.15 AM July 3rd. Company moved up via AVELUY WOOD - BLACK HORSE ROAD. Complete with 16 guns and Eight Officers. Crossing BLACK HORSE BRIDGE the company was heavily shelled proceeding to trench in village AUTHUILLE via evacuation trench. and moved from evacuation trench into village - west of CAMPBELL AVENUE (Map Ref 57 D SE. 20000 Q 36 c 22.) owing to heavy shelling, the company was compelled to lie down on coming out of trench for 15 mins. Company then proceeded along the sunken road 36 c 1 towards YATMAN BRIDGE.	
	3-7-16	1.30 AM	Heavy barrage of Artillery fire compelled the company to lie down again, one other rank was killed at this spot.	
		1.35 AM	2nd Lt. MURRAY was able to get through to Brigade Headquarters and report Company present. about 150 yds. away, and received orders for company to remain where they were. and await further orders.	
		4.30 AM	Until 4.30 AM the company remained under shelter in a ditch about 4'0 high - and at a low estimate about 20 H.E. Shells were dropped within a radius of about 1 acre	
		1.45 AM	Corpl Cochrane got through to Brigade HQ for details of attack and was informed attack has been postponed until 6.15 AM but to await final further orders	
		5.30 AM	Corpl. Cochrane received verbal orders to send 2 guns and teams to the 2nd S. Lancs. and 2 guns	

2449 Wt. W14957/M90 750,000 1/16 J.B.C. & A. Forms/C.2118/12.

INTELLIGENCE SUMMARY

(Erase heading not required.)

Place	Date	Hour	Summary of Events and Information	Remarks and references to Appendices
	3-7-16	5.30 AM	2 Guns and teams to the 11th Sholestires and 2 guns steams to the 8th Borderers to assist in the attack on Enemy Trenches named HINDENBURG TRENCH, running NE to SW R.31.c.68. to R.31.d.66. 2nd Lts BAILEY, COLLINGE, & MURRAY were detailed for this work, and proceeded under shell fire to positions allotted to them - 2nd Lts BAILEY & MURRAY and teams were successful in getting into the front line trench (W 36 d 94) - TYRONE STREET - 2nd Lt COLLINGE took up position in trench, BISSET STREET (W 36 B 8.4) and was able to give support. Unfortunately attack unsuccessful.	
		10 AM	O.C. 75 Co MGC Sent 2nd Lt H. JOHNSON with 2 guns up in case attack renewed. He took up position in INVERARY STREET. (W 36.6.8.6) on O.P. killed here. 2nd Lt MURRAY had 10 men wounded by a Shell & one gun buried. Enemy brought heavy fire to bear on this Sector. no dug outs, men + guns exposed.	
	night 3/4		Entire Company stood to - and all day of the 4th.	
	4-7-16	9pm	Company relieved by portion of the 147 Co. & part of 7th MGCo with great difficulty, men & guns were withdrawn and moved over AUTHUILLE BRIDGE to field (57°SE W10 b 6.4.) where they remained in the rain, exhausted by the trying ordeal.	
	5-7-16		Information recd that Company to go into billets to rest but order cancelled + Coy ordered to stand to. During 5th + 6th Coy stood to.	
	6-7-16		Company ordered to proceed to ALBERT.	
	7-7-16		A Section ordered to proceed to support 8th S. Lancs. in attack on village of OVILLIERS	
		6 pm	Remainder of Company ordered to move to USNA REDOUBT in support.	

INTELLIGENCE SUMMARY

(Erase heading not required.)

Place	Date	Hour	Summary of Events and Information	Remarks and references to Appendices
	7.7.16 8.7.16 9.7.16		Section under 2nd Lt BAILEY proceeded up captured Enemy trenches to front line to assist in attack on village. Two O.R. wounded. During morning LA BOISSELLE was reconnoitred by Capt Cochrane. 2nd Lt JOHNSON & MURRAY with a view to suppressing enemy M.G. fire from OVILLIERS, which was very active during night 8/9. - Positions were selected. 6 pm indirect fire brought to bear on Ovilliers. Range 2000 yds - which drew enemy fire. During Evening section in front line observed party of 20 enemy - M.G. brought to bear on them and only two of the party were not accounted for.	
	10.7.16		Section in front (captured enemy trench) discovered in an enemy M.G. Emplacement which had been demolished in the preliminary bombardment - an Enemy machine Gun & belt filling machine. 6. relief of the section by section under 2nd Lt JOHNSON & MURRAY. The Gun and belt filling machine were brought in to Coy H.Q.s The relieving section suffers heavily from Enemy shell fire whilst relieving.	
	11.7.16		Orders recd. from G.O.C. 75 Bgde. 4 Guns to be placed in position commanding MASH VALLEY & BAPAUME Rd. Guns placed under command of 2nd Lt BAILEY & VERNON.	
	12.7.16		Orders recd. fire to be opened + POZIERES ROAD traverses. Complied with & good results achieved.	
	13.7.16		Information recd. 2nd Lt H. JOHNSON wounded. 1 OR killed 2 OR wounded. 2nd Lt COLLINGE + 4 OR's sent up to replace Casualties. Positions of guns under 2nd Lt BAILEY & VERNON altered and indirect fire brought to bear on Enemy Communication & Support trenches - (G.O. G's orders).	
		9.30 A.M.	Sector of front line in which 4 guns were placed was heavily counter attacked. attack repulsed with heavy enemy losses.	
	14.7.16		4 Guns under 2nd Lt BAILEY & VERNON ordered by be moved to bring enfilade fire on Enemy communication trenches, in area over which attack timed for night of 14/15 to take place.	

INTELLIGENCE SUMMARY

(Erase heading not required.)

Place	Date	Hour	Summary of Events and Information	Remarks and references to Appendices
	14-7-16		By orders of G.O.C. 75th Inf. Brigade the 4 guns in the front line were withdrawn for purpose of bringing indirect fire on above named area. Guns safely withdrawn without casualties. +8 guns worked on area. 2nd Lt H. JOHNSON died of wounds.	
	15-7-16		Attack detailed for night 14/15 being not entirely successful indirect fire was maintained at intervals during the whole of this day. Company informed by Artillery F.O.O. he had seen bodies of Enemy troops scattered on POZIERES Rd by our indirect M.G. fire.	
	16-7-16		Orders rec'd that Coy was to be relieved on night of 16/17.	
	17-7-16	8 AM	Coy marched to SENLIS. All guns withdrawn without casualty.	
		10 AM	Arrived SENLIS. Left for HEDAUVILLE 5 pm. Arrived HEDAUVILLE 6.30 pm.	
	18-7-16	9 AM	Left HEDAUVILLE for AMPLIER arrived Camp there 3 pm.	
	19-7-16	3 pm	Inspection by Divisional General.	
	20-7-16		M.G. Training	
	21-7-16			
	22-7-16	9 AM	Left AMPLIER for VAUCHELLES L'AUTHIE arriving there at 1.45 pm.	
	23-7-16	11 AM	Left VAUCHELLES L'AUTHIE for ENGLEBELMER arriving there 3.45 pm.	
	24-7-16		Coy. overhauling guns and equipment.	
	25-7-16		Coy. left ENGLEBELMER and relieved the 35th Coy M.G.C. in AUCHONVILLIERS, 3 sections in the line one in reserve in MAILLY WOOD.	
	26-7-16		Bgde Sector issued N° 5 Emplacement at Knocke in + 2 O.R.s wounded.	
	27-7-16		Orders rec'd from Division to further reconnoitre Bde front. Carried out by Capt COCHRANE 2nd Lt BAILEY & MURRAY	

INTELLIGENCE SUMMARY

(Erase heading not required.)

Instructions regarding War Diaries and Intelligence Summaries are contained in F. S. Regs., Part II. and the Staff Manual respectively. Title Pages will be prepared in manuscript.

Place	Date	Hour	Summary of Events and Information	Remarks and references to Appendices
AUCHONVILLIERS	27-7-16		and a revised Scheme for defence drawn up –	
	25-7-16		Maps prepared and revised Scheme of defence completed and submitted to Brigade.	
	28-7-16		Fire was opened from 3a position at 9.30 AM on a scattered enemy working party who were not seen again. Indirect fire on enemy trenches also.	
	29-7-16		Various improvement to dug outs, trenches and Emplacements carried on. also loopholes at No 2 position was altered so as to arrow a traverse of about 65°	
	30-7-16		Fire was opened from No 7 alternative position on Waggon road E of BEAUMONT HAMEL also from 3 - 3a 1b position. Fire opened on enemy trenches from No 6.	
	31-7-16		No 2 Emplacement strengthened with Sandbags. Fire opened on new position in LANWICK St covering left flank. Gun moved from No 5 position to new position in LANWICK St covering left flank.	

75th Brigade.
25th Division.

75th BRIGADE

MACHINE GUN COMPANY

AUGUST 1 9 1 6

From O.C.
    75 Machine Gun Co⁷

To D.A.G.
    3rd Echelon.

    Herewith I send you War diary completed to Aug 31-16

                  Henry Bacon, Captain,
                      Commanding
                    75 MACHINE GUN COY

No. 75 MACHINE GUN COMPANY.
No. 1021
Date 4-9-16

WAR DIARY or INTELLIGENCE SUMMARY

75 M G Coy

Vol 4

Place	Date	Hour	Summary of Events and Information	Remarks and references to Appendices
AUCHONVILLERS	1-8-16		Situation quiet. Some shelling of our trenches between 9-10 pm. Sectoral relief No 4 relieving No 1 Section.	
"	2-8-16		Bearings of each emplacement and arcs of fire checked. Maps showing positions of all guns and arcs of fire prepared and submitted to H.Q. 75 Infantry Brigade. Indirect fire opened on enemy trenches during night. Enemy shelled AUCHONVILLERS intermittently all day. Instructions received that active operations in support of an attack to be made by the Anzac Corps would take place within 48 hours. Machine Guns of this Bn. to cooperate with enfilade fire on enemy trench system opposite Brigade front.	
"	3-8-16		Village of BEAUMONT HAMEL searched by direct fire in an endeavour to silence enemy machine guns which had been firing on our trenches. Guns moved into positions for active operations.	
"	4-8-16	9 pm	Operations ordered by 75 Infantry Brigade were carried out with apparently good results. Enemy retaliated with shrapnel fire over front and support lines.	
"	5-8-16		Work of strengthening and improving dug outs and machine gun emplacements.	
"	6-8-16		Sectoral relief. No 1 Section relieving No 2 Section. Village of BEAUMONT HAMEL and enemy trench system searched with machine gun fire.	

WAR DIARY
or
INTELLIGENCE SUMMARY

(Erase heading not required.)

Instructions regarding War Diaries and Intelligence Summaries are contained in F. S. Regs., Part II. and the Staff Manual respectively. Title Pages will be prepared in manuscript.

Place	Date	Hour	Summary of Events and Information	Remarks and references to Appendices
AUCHONVILLERS	7-8-16		During night 6/7 enemy machine guns displayed great activity. Our machine guns retaliated. Emplacements strengthened and improved.	
"	8-8-16		Fire was opened on suspected machine guns emplacements in BEAUMONT HAMEL. Enemy did not retaliate. Information received that this Coy would be relieved on Aug 9-16 by the 2nd Guards Brigade Machine Gun Coy.	
"	9-8-16		Relief orders issued and relief completed. Company marched to ST LEGER-les-AUTHIE.	
ST LEGER-LES-AUTHIE	10-8-16	2. am	Company arrived. Company paid. Instructions received that Company was to proceed to AUTHIE. Company left ST LEGER-LES-AUTHIE at 2 pm arrived at AUTHIE. 3 pm	
AUTHIE	11-8-16		General work of overhauling and checking contents of limbers and work on training area.	
"	12-8-16		Capt F. E. C. Bacon arrived. Instructions received from 75 Infantry Brigade that Capt Bacon was to take over command of the Company from Capt R Cochrane. Coy worked on training area.	
"	13-8-16		Command of Coy formally handed over to Capt Bacon. Church parade and routine work.	

WAR DIARY
or
INTELLIGENCE SUMMARY

(Erase heading not required.)

Instructions regarding War Diaries and Intelligence Summaries are contained in F.S. Regs., Part II. and the Staff Manual respectively. Title Pages will be prepared in manuscript.

Place	Date	Hour	Summary of Events and Information	Remarks and references to Appendices
HEDAUVILLE	20-8-16		Church parade and routine work. No 1 section returned from AUTHUILLE WOOD	
"	21-8-16 } 25-8-16		Coy Training on area.	
"	26-8-16		Instructions received that a section was to relieve section of 7th Machine Gun Coy in LEIPZIG SALIENT. No 3 Section under Lt W. MILNE proceeded and relief of section carried out. Remainder of Coy stood by at HEDAUVILLE. 1 OR killed. 3 OR wounded.	
"	27-8-16	8a- 10p-	Coy ordered to relieve 7th Machine Gun Coy. Coy left HEDAUVILLE. Relief of 7th Machine Gun Coy completed.	
AUTHUILLE	28-8-16		Coy arrived AUTHUILLE. To assist attack on enemy trenches in the LEIPZIG SALIENT, the guns of Coy carried out indirect and enfilade fire on enemy trench system. Enemy retaliated with heavy shrapnel fire. 2 OR killed. 1 wounded.	
"	29-8-16		Enemy shelled our front and support trenches heavily. Indirect and enfilade fire as on 28th. 2 OR killed.	
"	30-8-16		Indirect and enfilade fire as on previous days. Sectional relief No 1 section relieving No 3 Section. Gap in enemy trench kept under fire by gun under command of Lt N.P. BAILEY.	
"	31-8-16		Enemy shelled our front and support trenches. Casualty 1 OR killed. Indirect fire as before.	

75th. INFANTRY BDE.

25th. DIVISION

75th. MACHINE GUN COMPANY

SEPTEMBER 1916.

75th. INFANTRY BDE.

25th. DIVISION

Army Form C. 2118.

Vol 5
25

WAR DIARY
or
INTELLIGENCE SUMMARY.
(Erase heading not required.)

...75 Machine Gun Company.

Instructions regarding War Diaries and Intelligence Summaries are contained in F.S. Regs., Part II. and the Staff Manual respectively. Title pages will be prepared in manuscript.

Place	Date	Hour	Summary of Events and Information	Remarks and references to Appendices
AUTHUILLE	1-9-16		Preparations made for attack on trenches in the LEIPZIG SALIENT. Attack postponed until 3rd. Indirect and enfilade fire carried out by all available guns on enemy trench system. Gaps in enemy trenches fired on at intervals during night.	
"	2-9-16		Indirect and enfilade fire on enemy trench system.	
"	3-9-16	5.10 am	Attack on enemy trench in LEIPZIG SALIENT. Infantry reached their objective but same could not be retained owing to heavy counter attacks and the prior evacuation of trench captured. Enemy shelled front and support trenches also village of AUTHUILLE heavily with shrapnel and H.E. shells.	
"	4-9-16		Indirect and enfilade fire on enemy communication trenches. Our trench system shelled. 2 O.R. wounded.	
"	5-9-16		Indirect and enfilade fire on enemy trenches. Our front and support lines shelled heavily.	
"	6-9-16		Indirect and enfilade fire as on previous days. AUTHUILLE shelled heavily during night. 6/T. Lt. N.P. BAILEY wounded but remained at duty.	
"	7-9-16		Instructions received that 32nd Machine Gun Co would relieve this Co. Relief accomplished and Co withdrawn to SOUTH BLUFF, Beach Horse Bridge. 2 O.R. killed.	
SOUTH BLUFF	8-9-16		Co left 9 a.m. for LEALVILLERS.	

T2134. Wt. W708—776. 500000. 4/15. Sir J. C. & S.

Army Form C. 2118.

WAR DIARY
or
INTELLIGENCE SUMMARY.
(Erase heading not required.)

75 Machine Gun Coy.

Instructions regarding War Diaries and Intelligence Summaries are contained in F. S. Regs., Part II. and the Staff Manual respectively. Title pages will be prepared in manuscript.

Place	Date	Hour	Summary of Events and Information	Remarks and references to Appendices
LEALVILLERS	8-9-16	5 p.m.	Company arrived at LEALVILLERS.	
"	9-9-16		Checking contents of limbers, cleaning guns and equipment	
"	10-9-16	7.30 a.m.	Company left for ORVILLE 7.30 a.m.	
ORVILLE	"	1 p.m.	Company arrived at ORVILLE 1 p.m.	
"	11-9-16	8.0 a.m.	Company left for BOISBERGUES	
BOISBERGUES	"	2.0 p.m.	Company arrived BOISBERGUES	
"	12-9-16	8.0 a.m.	Company left for CRAMONT.	
CRAMONT	"	1 p.m.	Company arrived CRAMONT.	
"	13-9-16		Company refitting checking contents of limbers and cleaning guns and equipments	
"	14-9-16 to 23-9-16		Company training on training area.	
"	24-9-16		Instructions received that Coy would move to AMPLIER on 25th and from AMPLIER to ARQUEVES on 26th.	
"	25-9-16	8-0 a.m.	Company left CRAMONT	
AMPLIER	"	3-0 p.m.	Company arrived. Instructions received that Coy would move to LEALVILLERS instead of ARQUEVES on 26th.	

Army Form C. 2118.

WAR DIARY
or
INTELLIGENCE SUMMARY
(Erase heading not required.)

75 Machine Gun Co Y.

Instructions regarding War Diaries and Intelligence Summaries are contained in F. S. Regs., Part II. and the Staff Manual respectively. Title Pages will be prepared in manuscript.

Place	Date	Hour	Summary of Events and Information	Remarks and references to Appendices
AMPLIER	26-9-16	10.0am	Co Y left. On march destination of Co Y was changed to ACHEUX.	
ACHEUX	"	1.0pm	Co Y arrived.	
"	27-9-16 / 28-9-16		Co Y equipment prepared for active operations.	
"	29-9-16	7.0am	Co Y left.	
BOUZINCOURT	"	10.0am	Co Y arrived and bivouacs erected for night 29/30 Sept.	
"	30-9-16	8.0am	Co Y left and took over section of line between OVILLERS and POZIERES from 32nd machine gun Co Y. Sections heavily shelled. 1 OR killed. 3 OR wounded.	

75th INFANTRY BDE
25th DIVISION.

75th MACHINE GUN COMPANY

OCTOBER   1916

From O.C.
  75 Machine Gun Co.

To H.Q.
  75 Brigade.

Herewith please find original War Diary for month of October 1916.

　　　　　　　　J. H. Dailey　Lt.
　　　　　　　　　　O/C
　　　　　　　　　　75 M.G. Coy

No. 75 MACHINE GUN COMPANY
No. 1280
Date 2-11-16

WAR DIARY or INTELLIGENCE SUMMARY

Army Form C. 2118.

75 Machine Gun Co.

Vol.

Place	Date	Hour	Summary of Events and Information	Remarks and references to Appendices
POZIERES	1-10-16		Support lines heavily shelled by enemy. Guns moved from STUFF REDOUBT to HESSIAN TRENCH.	
"	2-10-16		Front and support lines heavily shelled by enemy guns rearranged and alternative positions reconnoitred. Indirect fire on enemy trench system.	
"	3-10-16		Indirect fire on enemy trench system. Two guns fired on enemy working parties who scattered and were not seen again.	
"	4-10-16		Indirect fire on enemy trench system.	
"	5-10-16		Indirect fire on enemy trench system.	
"	6-10-16	1.0 p.m.	Company relieved by 74th Machine Gun Co. and marched into camp near BOUZINCOURT.	
BOUZINCOURT	7-10-16		To assist proposed operations by Canadian Division No. 3 section, 4 guns under Lt W. MILNE left for MOUQUET FARM to assist 74th Machine Gun Co. in carrying out indirect fire on enemy trench system. 1 O.R. killed. Remaining 3 sections of Company checking contents of limbers and cleaning guns and equipment.	
"	8-10-16		Company training	
"	9-10-16		Company training	
"	10-10-16		Company training	
"	11-10-16		Company training	

Army Form C. 2118.

75 Machine Gun Co^y

WAR DIARY
or
INTELLIGENCE SUMMARY.
(Erase heading not required.)

Instructions regarding War Diaries and Intelligence Summaries are contained in F. S. Regs., Part II. and the Staff Manual respectively. Title pages will be prepared in manuscript.

Place	Date	Hour	Summary of Events and Information	Remarks and references to Appendices
BOUZINCOURT	12-10-16	10·0 a·m·	The operations by Canadian divisions having concluded N° 3 section under Lt W. Milne returned from Mouquet Farm. Company cleaning guns and training	
	13-10-16		Company training	
	14-10-16		Company training	
	15-10-16	8·0 a·m·	Company left camp and marched to positions N of Ovillers relieving the 7th Machine gun company in the line. Company H.Q being at X 9.b.0.4. Sheet 57 d SE 1-20000	
Point X 2.b.0.4	16-10-16		Indirect fire on enemy trench system. Guns in front line fired several times at good targets with excellent results.	
	17-10-16		In anticipation of active operations, work was commenced on a new trench from which overhead fire could be directed on enemy communication trenches N of Regina Trench. 1 O.R. wounded. Section of 7th Machine Gun Co^y was attached to this company and carried out overhead fire on enemy positions. These guns were posted in Skyline Trench.	
	18-10-16		Instructions received from C.O. 75th Infantry Brigade that 2 positions on the right of line at present held were to be taken over by this Co^y. Arrangements made and positions taken over. Indirect fire carried out from positions in Skyline Trench and other positions. Work on new indirect fire trench continued and emplacements built	

Army Form C. 2118.

WAR DIARY
or
INTELLIGENCE SUMMARY.
(Erase heading not required.)

75 Machine Gun Coy

Place	Date	Hour	Summary of Events and Information	Remarks and references to Appendices
Pozt X2 & u	18.10.16		Information received that 75 Infantry Brigade would attack REGINA TRENCH, STUMP R.D and STUFF TRENCH on the 19th at an hour which would be notified later. Preparations were therefore made to assist the assault by bursts of fire on enemy communication trenches and STUMP R.D	
Sheet 57d S.E.	19.10.16		Owing to heavy rain attack postponed until 20th. Work was therefore continued on indirect fire trench which was deepened and gun emplacements strengthened. Indirect fire carried out as on previous days.	
	20.10.16		Attack postponed until 21st. Advantage was taken of this postponement and gun emplacements were further strengthened. Enemy shelled our front and support line positions vigorously.	
	21.10.16	5.0am	Enemy attacked SCHWABEN TRENCH but were repelled. Direct fire was used on enemy accumulating. Infantry with foot mounts attack on REGINA TRENCH by 75 Infantry Brigade timed for 12.06 pm. Attack was entirely successful. The whole objective was gained and consolidated. Indirect fire was carried out prior to the attack and after objective had been gained. 14 guns were employed at this work. During to enemy trenches being out of range from SKYLINE TRENCH the 4 guns of the 7th Machine Gun Coy were withdrawn.	
		11.0pm	Information received that advanced posts had been established in R.22.b, R.16.c and R.15.a. Overhead fire was therefore stopped.	

Army Form C. 2118.

WAR DIARY
or
INTELLIGENCE SUMMARY.
(Erase heading not required.)

75 Machine Gun Co?

Place	Date	Hour	Summary of Events and Information	Remarks and references to Appendices
X2604	22.10.16	2.0pm	Company relieved and marched into camp near BOUZINCOURT	
BOUZINCOURT	23.10.16	1.0pm	Company left for WARLOY	
WARLOY		4.0pm	Company arrived and settled in billets	
	24.10.16	7.0am	Company left for AUTHIEULE via LEALVILLERS, SARTON and AMPLIER.	
AUTHIEULE		2.0pm	Company arrived	
	25.10.16		Company refitting, checking contents of limbers, cleaning guns and equipment.	
	26.10.16		Company training	
	27.10.16		-do-	
	28.10.16		-do-	
	29.10.16	3.45pm	Information received that Company was to entrain at DOULLENS station for BAILLEUL	
		6.10pm	No 1 Section entrained at Doullens station on arrival at BAILLEUL marched to METEREN	
		9.10pm	No 2 Section -do-	
	30.10.16	12.10am	No 3 Section -do-	
		3.10am	No 4 Section -do-	
METEREN	31.10.16		Company route march. Lt N.P. BAILEY reconnoitred line to be taken over by this Company	

75th Inf. Bde.

25th Division

75th MACHINE GUN COMPANY,

NOVEMBER, 1916.

| No. 75 |
| MACHINE GUN |
| COMPANY. |

No. 1386
Date 1-12-16

From O.C.
   75 Machine Gun Coy

To H.Q.
   75 Brigade

   Herewith please find Original War diary completed to Nov 30 1916.

Henry Bacon
Major
Cdg 75 M.G.Cy

Army Form C. 2118.

WAR DIARY
or
INTELLIGENCE SUMMARY.
(Erase heading not required.)

75 Machine Gun Coy

Instructions regarding War Diaries and Intelligence Summaries are contained in F. S. Regs., Part II. and the Staff Manual respectively. Title pages will be prepared in manuscript.

Place	Date	Hour	Summary of Events and Information	Remarks and references to Appendices
METEREN	1-11-16	7.45a	Company left METEREN	
LE ROMARIN	2-11-16	11.0a.m	Company arrived at ROMARIN. Arrangements for relief of 9/5 Machine Gun Coy completed	
"	2-11-16		Relief of 91st Machine Gun Coy completed. Headquarters established at VICKERS CAMP, LE ROMARIN, B.4.c.3.9. Sheet 36 NW 1:20000. Advanced Headquarters at CHATEAU LA HUTTE U.14.c.1.4. Sheet 28 SW 1:20000	
"	3-11-16		Indirect fire on SCHNITZEL FARM and MESSINES Rd. Enemy machine guns active.	
"	4-11-16		Indirect fire on enemy trench system. Special attention being paid to trench junctions. During night 4/5 our guns did not fire owing to our patrols and working parties being out all night.	
"	5-11-16		Indirect fire on enemy trench system. Very quiet all day. Some M.G. activity during evening	
"	6-11-16		Enemy machine guns active. Our guns fired on enemy trench system.	
"	7-11-16		Sectional relief. Indirect fire on MESSINES Rd and AVENUE FARM.	
"	8-11-16		Indirect fire on enemy trench system. Enemy machine guns retaliated. To assist information finds to commence at 4.30 a.m. No 9 & 3 Gun and teams were moved up from Company HQ. at LE ROMARIN to the CHATEAU LA HUTTE	

Army Form C. 2118.

WAR DIARY
or
INTELLIGENCE SUMMARY.
(Erase heading not required.)

Instructions regarding War Diaries and Intelligence Summaries are contained in F.S. Regs., Part II. and the Staff Manual respectively. Title pages will be prepared in manuscript.

Place	Date	Hour	Summary of Events and Information	Remarks and references to Appendices
LE ROMARIN	9-11-16	4.30 a	Indirect and searching fire on MESSINES Rᴅ. SCHNITZEL FARM, AVENUE FARM and on enemy trenches near TILLEUL FARM and LA DOUVE FARM. Fire was maintained until 4.50 a.m. Enemy retaliated with a few high velocity shells on our front line. Rest of day quiet. During evening bursts on enemy trench system were fired on.	
	10-11-16		Indirect fire on suspected machine gun emplacements in enemy lines. Preparations made for operations timed to commence 10 p.m. These operations were subsequently cancelled.	
	11-11-16		Instructions received from G.O.C. 75th Infantry Brigade that operations postponed from 10th would be carried out at 10.10 p.m. This instruction was carried out and points selected were fired on.	
	12-11-16		Sectional relief. Enemy trenches, aeroplane and trench junctions fired on.	
	13-11-16		Indirect fire on SCHNITZEL FARM and MESSINES Rᴅ. Enemy medium guns were particularly predictive during night.	
	14-11-16		Indirect fire on MESSINES Rᴅ. SCHNITZEL FARM, ASH AVENUE, TILLEUL FARM, LE POTTERIE FARM. Enemy fired a few high velocity shells in the vicinity of MAD'T RUIN.	
	15-11-16		Indirect fire on MESSINES Rᴅ and ROADSIDE REDOUBT.	
	16-11-16		Indirect fire from guns of HASTED HOUSE on Road junction. U.3.a.25.20 and guns at CHATEAU LA HUTTE fired on road U.2.d.45.70 to 90.90. Sheet Sᵗ 28 NW 1-20000	

Army Form C. 2118.

WAR DIARY
or
INTELLIGENCE SUMMARY.
(Erase heading not required.)

Instructions regarding War Diaries and Intelligence Summaries are contained in F. S. Regs., Part II. and the Staff Manual respectively. Title pages will be prepared in manuscript.

75 Machine Gun Co.

Place	Date	Hour	Summary of Events and Information	Remarks and references to Appendices
LE ROMARIN	17-11-16		Sectional relief. In connection with operations ordered by G.O.C. 75 Infantry Brigade, indirect fire was carried out on LA PETIT DOUVE FARM, MESSINES R⁴, enemy communication trenches and GREY FARM.	
	18-11-16		Indirect fire on LA PETIT DOUVE FARM, MESSINES R⁴ and AVENUE FARM.	
	19-11-16		Indirect fire on LA POTTERIE FARM, AU BON FERMIER CAB⁴ and enemy communication trenches. Enemy shelled CHATEAU LA HUTTE and STABLE FORT with 5.9's but little damage resulted.	
	20-11-16		During day situation quiet. Enemy machine guns were active during evening and at intervals during night. Indirect fire was carried out on selected points in enemy trench system.	
	21-11-16		Situation normal. Indirect fire on AVENUE FARM and opposite M.G. emplacements.	
	22-11-16		Sectional relief. Fired on SCHNITZEL FARM, AVENUE FARM, TILLEUL FARM and Sundries round LA DOUVE FARM.	
	23-11-16		Quiet day. Fired on LA PETIT DOUVE FARM, and on junction in enemy trench system.	
	24-11-16		Situation normal. Fired on LA PETIT DOUVE FARM, and SCHNITZEL FARM. Slight enemy artillery activity.	
	25-11-16		Enemy shelled CHATEAU LA HUTTE from 9 to 10 a.m. About 90 shells were counted. Guns at BACK ESTAMINET fired on ROADSIDE REDOUBT. In accordance with 75 Brigade Order 119 fire was directed upon enemy communication trenches to right and left of LA DOUVE FARM, MESSINES R⁴. Trenches around GREY FARM and trenches leading to TILLEUL FARM. Firing commenced firing at 6 p.m. 25th. Ceased 3 a.m. 26th.	

T2134. Wt. W708—776. 500000. 4/16. Sir J. C. & S.

Army Form C. 2118.

WAR DIARY
or
INTELLIGENCE SUMMARY.
(Erase heading not required.)

7S Machine Gun Coy

Instructions regarding War Diaries and Intelligence Summaries are contained in F. S. Regs., Part II. and the Staff Manual respectively. Title pages will be prepared in manuscript.

Place	Date	Hour	Summary of Events and Information	Remarks and references to Appendices
LE ROMARIN	26-11-16		Enemy artillery active between 11 and 11.30 a.m. E. shells fell in the vicinity of the CHATEAU LA HUTTE. 2 direct hits on machine gun emplacements at CHATEAU and STABLE FORT. Enemy Machine guns were active during evening. Our guns fired on ROADSIDE REDOUBT.	
	27-11-16		Situation very quiet all day. Practically no enemy activity.	
	28-11-16		No enemy activity. Emplacements repaired and improved. Trenches sandbagged.	
	29-11-16		Situation generally quiet. Guns fired on SCHNITZEL FARM, LA PETIT DOUVE FARM, and MESSINES R.R.	

75th Inf. Bde.

25th Division

75th MACHINE GUN COMPANY,

<u>D E C E M B E R,   1 9 1 6</u>.

Army Form C. 2118.

WAR DIARY
or
INTELLIGENCE SUMMARY.
(Erase heading not required.)

75 Machine Gun Coy.

Vol 8

Instructions regarding War Diaries and Intelligence Summaries are contained in F.S. Regs., Part II. and the Staff Manual respectively. Title pages will be prepared in manuscript.

Place	Date	Hour	Summary of Events and Information	Remarks and references to Appendices
ROMARIN	1-12-16		Generally quiet but some artillery and machine gun activity during night. Coy guns fired on LA PETIT DOUVE FARM, ASH AVENUE, LA POTTERIE FARM and MESSINES RD.	
-do-	2-12-16		Sectional relief. Indirect fire on LA PETIT DOUVE FARM.	
-do-	3-12-16		Indirect fire on LA PETIT DOUVE FARM and SCHNITZEL FARM. Instructions received from G.O.C. 75 Infantry Brigade that this Coy would be relieved in sector at present held on Dec 4 and 5 by 109 Machine Gun Coy and a new sector taken over from SUFFOLK AVE (exclusive) to STRAND (exclusive) in relief of portions of 7 and 74 Machine Gun Coys. Details of relief to be arranged between O's Coy. Machine Gun Coys concerned.	
-do-	4-12-16		Positions at GERMAN HOUSE, READING FORT, BACK HOUSE and FORT WALTER taken over from 74 Machine Gun Coy. Advanced Coy HQ established in PLOEGSTEERT WOOD	
-do-	5-12-16		Relief of Coy by 109 Machine Gun Coy completed as per arrangements made. Enemy artillery and machine guns active. Twelve 5.9" shells fell in vicinity of FORT READING.	
-do-	6-12-16		Enemy trench mortars and machine guns active. A searchlight from an enemy position on the BIRDCAGE searched vicinity of GERMAN HOUSE. Guns at FORT READING fired on enemy trenches, railway and road near PONT ROUGE.	
-do-	7-12-16		Enemy snipers, machine guns and trench mortars active. We fired on LA PETIT HAIE FARM.	

Army Form C. 2118.

WAR DIARY
or
INTELLIGENCE SUMMARY.
(Erase heading not required.)

Instructions regarding War Diaries and Intelligence Summaries are contained in F. S. Regs., Part II. and the Staff Manual respectively. Title pages will be prepared in manuscript.

75 Machine Gun Co?

Place	Date	Hour	Summary of Events and Information	Remarks and references to Appendices
ROMARIN	8-12-16		Enemy trench mortars active. A number of rifle grenades fell in vicinity of FORT WALTER. Indirect fire on enemy trenches road, railway and bridge around PONT ROUGE.	
"	9-12-16		Enemy trench mortars active around GERMAN HOUSE. Enemy fired a number of rifle grenades at emplacements near FORT WALTER. Enemy snipers and machine guns also active. PONT ROUGE fired on.	
"	10-12-16		Enemy artillery and machine guns active. BACK HOUSE and vicinity shelled. 2 O.R. killed. We fired on LA PETIT HAIE FARM and on railway, road, trenches and bridge at PONT ROUGE.	
"	11-12-16		Situation generally quiet but some enemy machine gun fire during night. We fired on usual targets around PONT ROUGE also on junctions in enemy trench system.	
"	12-12-16		Enemy machine guns active during night otherwise situation quiet. Communication trench from LOOPHOLE FARM (U 22 d 1.2) to U 23 c 9.9. Sheet 28 S.W. 1-20000.	
"	13-12-16		Situation quiet. We fired on PETIT HAIE FARM also on selected points in enemy trench system.	
"	14-12-16		Situation normal. Indirect fire on PONT ROUGE and enemy C.T's from U 29 a 7.8 to U 29 b 0.5.90 and from U 29 b 1.9 to U 29 b 6.4. Sheet 28 S.W. 1-20000. U 22 d 7.0 was also fired on at same distance as enemy had been observed at this point at this time on previous days.	
"	15-12-16		Enemy artillery active. Shells fell in vicinity of BACK HOUSE. We fired on usual targets around PONT ROUGE.	

Army Form C. 2118.

75 Machine Gun Co?

WAR DIARY
or
INTELLIGENCE SUMMARY.
(Erase heading not required.)

Instructions regarding War Diaries and Intelligence Summaries are contained in F. S. Regs., Part II. and the Staff Manual respectively. Title pages will be prepared in manuscript.

Place	Date	Hour	Summary of Events and Information	Remarks and references to Appendices
ROMARIN	16-12-16		Enemy machine guns and snipers active. Indirect fire on PONT ROUGE and junctions in enemy trench system.	
"	17-12-16		Enemy machine guns and snipers active. We fired on PETIT HAIE FARM and PONT ROUGE.	
"	18-12-16		Usual activity by enemy machine guns and snipers. Fired on enemy trenches on LOOPHOLE FARM.	
"	19-12-16		Enemy shelled vicinity of CONVENT. We fired on bridge and trenches around PONT ROUGE.	
"	20-12-16		Enemy machine guns and snipers particularly active. We fired on PONT ROUGE and vicinity.	
"	21-12-16		Enemy artillery active during afternoon. Several high velocity shells fell near LANCASHIRE SUPPORT FARM. We fired on gap cut in enemy wire by our artillery also on enemy machine gun at U 28 a 4.8. Sheet 28 S.W. 1-20000.	
"	22-12-16		Enemy artillery and Trench mortars active. Indirect fire on junctions in enemy trench system also on PONT ROUGE and PETIT HAIE FARM.	
"	23-12-16		Enemy artillery and Trench mortars active. We fired on SOUTH face of BIRDCAGE also on enemy wire at U 28 d 4.8. Usual indirect fire on PONT ROUGE and vicinity.	
"	24-12-16		Enemy artillery, machine guns and snipers active. Concrete emplacement at BURNT OUT FARM and LANCASHIRE SUPPORT FARM hit by enemy shells. We fired on U 28 a 4.8 and usual targets in PONT ROUGE.	

T2134. Wt. W708-776. 500000. 4/15. Sir J. C. & S.

Army Form C. 2118.

WAR DIARY
or
INTELLIGENCE SUMMARY.
(Erase heading not required.)

75 Machine Gun Co.

Place	Date	Hour	Summary of Events and Information	Remarks and references to Appendices
ROMARIN	25/12/16		Situation normal. Some enemy machine gun activity during evening. We fired on enemy front line also on PONT ROUGE and LA PETIT HAIE FARM.	
	26/12/16		Enemy artillery and trench mortars active. Vicinity of BACK HOUSE shelled and part of LOWNDES AVE blown in. We fired direct on enemy M.G. at U 28 a 4.8 also on part of front line. Indirect fire on targets near U 23 a 9.9. Enemy LT's from LOOPHOLE FARM to U 23 a 8.3. PONT ROUGE and vicinity.	
	27/12/16		Enemy artillery trench mortars and machine guns active. We fired on usual targets around PONT ROUGE also on PETIT HAIE FARM and enemy communication trenches.	
	28/12/16		Enemy artillery. Trench mortars and snipers active. Several shells fell in vicinity of BACK HOUSE. We fired on usual targets.	
	29/12/16		Usual activity on part of the enemy. Firing was carried out on targets indicated in 75 Brigade Order No 129.	
	30/12/16		Usual firing on PETIT HAIE FARM and PONT ROUGE.	
	31/12/16		Instructions received from 75 Infantry Brigade that Co¹ would be relieved on the line on Jan 1. 1917. details of relief to be arranged between Officers commanding. We fired on GRAND HAIE and PETIT HAIE FARMS. Halt at U 23 a 90.95 and bridge at PONT ROUGE.	

Army Form C. 2118.

WAR DIARY
or
INTELLIGENCE SUMMARY.
(Erase heading not required.)

75 M.G.Co.

Place	Date	Hour	Summary of Events and Information	Remarks and references to Appendices
ROMARIN	1-1-17		Company relieved by 195 Machine Gun Co.	
	2-1-17	10.0am	Company left.	
CATTERS CAMP DE SEULE	3-1-17	11:30am	Company arrived. Cleaning and checking contents of limbers. Limbers thoroughly overhauled. All equipment cleaned. Programme of training and classes for Signallers. Range takers and partially trained men arranged.	
"	4-1-17		Nº 1 Section firing on range at MONT DE LILLE. Partially trained men, signallers and range takers under instructors. Lecture by Section officer on "MAP READING"	
"	5-1-17		Orders/Instructions received from G.O.C. 75 Infantry Brigade. Major H.E.C. Bacon left for U.K. Lt N.P. BAILEY took over command of Co. All sections advanced drill on training area	
"	6-1-17		Nº 2 Section on range. All other men advanced drill on Training area except range takers. Signallers and partially trained men who were under instructors	
"	7-1-17		Church parade and sports	
"	8-1-17		Nº 3 Section on range. Signallers, range takers and partially trained men under instructors. Remainder of Co. advanced drill on training area	
"	9-1-17		4 Section attached to 11 Bn Cheshire Regt. Remainder advanced drill on training area. Lecture and squad drill in afternoon	

WAR DIARY or INTELLIGENCE SUMMARY

Army Form C. 2118.

75 M.G.C'i

Place	Date	Hour	Summary of Events and Information	Remarks and references to Appendices
CARTERS CAMP DE SEULE	10-7-17		Advanced drill on Training area. Recce 1 section, 2 range finders and 2 of rallies attached 1/5 2 Bn South Lance Regt. Lecture and squad drill in afternoon.	
"	11-7-17		No 4 section 1 section, 2 range takers and 2 of rallies attached to 8 Bn South Lance Regt. Remainder advanced drill on Training area. Lectures and squad drill in afternoon.	
"	12-7-17		Advanced drill on Training area. Recce 1 section, 2 range takers and 2 of rallies attached to 8 Bn Border Regt. Lecture and squad drill in afternoon.	
"	13-7-17		The Company took part in attack practice under 75 Infantry Brigade arrangements.	
"	14-7-17		Divine service and recreation	
"	15-7-17		Attack practice on Training area	
"	16-7-17		Instructions received that this Co.y would relieve 7 Machine Gun Co.y in the line under arrangements to be made between Co. & Bg. Details of relief arranged and company left CARTERS Camp at 1.0 p.m.	
LE BIZET	17-7-17	3.15	Co.y arrived at position at LYS FARM. Relieve night 16/17 and 10 guns taken into line same night. Relief of 7 machine gun Co.y completed. HQ established at LE BIZET C 13 d 2.7 Sheet 36 NW with Trench HQ at RESERVE F.M. L 3 A 7.1 and LE TOUQUET S'n Cq d 8.7.	

Army Form C. 2118.

75 M. G. Cᵒʸ

WAR DIARY
or
INTELLIGENCE SUMMARY.
(Erase heading not required.)

Instructions regarding War Diaries and Intelligence Summaries are contained in F. S. Regs., Part II. and the Staff Manual respectively. Title pages will be prepared in manuscript.

Place	Date	Hour	Summary of Events and Information	Remarks and references to Appendices
LE BIZET	18-1-17		Enemy artillery and trench mortars active. We fired on FRELINGHIEN and TWIN COTS.	
"	19-1-17		Enemy trench mortars active. Several fell in vicinity of our gun positions. Some shells fell near light railway close to POMPADOUR FARM. We fired on points in enemy CT's	
"	20-1-17		Enemy artillery, trench mortars and machine guns active. We fired on FRELINGHIEN.	
"	21-1-17		Situation generally quiet but some trench mortar activity. We fired on TWIN COTS and points in FRELINGHIEN.	
"	22-1-17		Enemy artillery and trench mortar activity especially between 1.45 and 6 pm BARKENHAM Ave rendered impassable. We fired on bridge and trenches around FRELINGHIEN. Crossroads at C.11.b.3.9 and bridges over river LYS at C5a.3.9 and 3.5. HOUPLINES Sheet 1:10000.	
"	23-1-17		Enemy artillery very active from 2 pm. About 5 pm enemy attempted to raid our trenches near LE GHEER RD but were driven back. Artillery fire intense and portions of our trench system were destroyed. Our guns opened barrage fire on No Man's Land and enemy CT's in response to SOS signal. During night we carried out indirect fire on Cross roads at C11.b.3.9. Bridges over river LYS at C5a.3.3 + 3.5 and vicinity. UMPIRE DRIVE U.22.d. also on points in FRELINGHIEN.	

Army Form C. 2118.

75 M G C?

WAR DIARY
or
INTELLIGENCE SUMMARY.
(Erase heading not required.)

Place	Date	Hour	Summary of Events and Information	Remarks and references to Appendices
LE BIZET	24-1-17		Enemy artillery and trench mortars active especially from noon until 5 p.m. Indirect fire was carried out in accordance with instructions contained in 75 Infantry Brigade Order 139. Following trenches and tracks were fired on. Enemy support line from CROWN PRINCE FARM to TWIN COTS. C.T. from CROWN PRINCE FARM to river LYS. C.T's and tracks between TWIN COTS and WHITE F.M. At intervals during night 23/24 following points were fired on. Bridges over river LYS at C5a 3.3 + 3.5. Boxcarado at C11 b 3.9. FRELINGHIEN. Several heavy shells (apparently 21 cm) fell in LE BIZET at C13 b 8.2 and 5.0. between 2.30 + 9.30 p.m.	
"	25-1-17		Enemy artillery and trench mortars active also enemy machine guns during night about 20 H.V. shells fell in vicinity of LE TOUQUET ST? but no damage resulted. Indirect fire on following targets at intervals during night. Bridge over river LYS at C11 a 4.5.15. Bridges at C5 a 3.3 + 3.5. Boxcarado at C11 b 3.9. C.T. from CROWN PRINCE F.M. to bridge at C11 a 4.5.15. FRELINGHIEN.	
"	26-1-17		Situation normal but enemy machine guns were active during night. Weather very cold. Guns were therefore fired at short intervals to prevent freezing. Indirect fire was carried out on C.T. leading from CROWN PRINCE FARM to bridge over river LYS at C11 a 5.2. Support trench from TWIN COTS to CROWN PRINCE F.M. Bridge over river LYS at C5 a 3.3 and 3.5. FRELINGHIEN.	

Army Form C. 2118.

WAR DIARY
or
INTELLIGENCE SUMMARY.
(Erase heading not required.)

75 M.G.C.

Instructions regarding War Diaries and Intelligence Summaries are contained in F.S. Regs., Part II. and the Staff Manual respectively. Title pages will be prepared in manuscript.

Place	Date	Hour	Summary of Events and Information	Remarks and references to Appendices
LE BIZET	27-1-17		Situation generally quiet but enemy machine guns were active at intervals. Weather cold and frosty. Guns were therefore fired frequently. Indirect fire on Bridge over river LYS at C5a 3.3 and 3.5. FRELINGHIEN. Cross roads at C11 b. 3.9. C.T. leading from CROWN PRINCE F.M. to Bridge over river LYS at C11a 5.2.	
"	28-1-17		Enemy artillery active. LONG AVE 2Bsun.m. near RIGHT SECTOR H.Q. Enemy machine guns and trench mortars also active. Indirect fire on Bridge over river LYS at C5a 3.3 & 3.5 and tracks leading to them. Track from TWIN COTS to WHITE F.M. C.T. from CROWN PRINCE F.M. to Bridge over river LYS at C11a S.2. FRELINGHIEN. Main St and church square.	
"	29-1-17		Situation normal. Indirect fire on cross roads at C11 b - 3.9. Bridge over river LYS at C5a 3.3. 3.5. UMPIRE DRIVE, U.22.d. FRELINGHIEN Church square.	
"	30-1-17		Situation generally quiet but enemy machine guns were active at intervals. Weather cold. Guns fired at intervals to prevent freezing. Indirect fire on FRELINGHIEN bridges over river LYS at C5a 3.3 and 3.5. Cross roads at C11 b. 3.9	
"	31-1-17		Enemy artillery French mortars and machine guns active. Weather frosty. Guns were fired at intervals. Indirect fire on enemy support line from CROWN PRINCE F.M. to TWIN COTS. Bridges over river LYS at C5a 3.3 & 3.5. Bridge over river LYS at C11 a 4.5.15. FRELINGHIEN.	

From O.C.
  75 Machine Gun Co.

To H.Q.
  75 Brigade

  Herewith please find original War Diary completed to Feb 28-17.

> No. 75
> MACHINE GUN
> COMPANY.
> No. 1814
> Date 1-3-17

    Wm Milne Captain.
    Commanding
    75 MACHINE GUN COY

WAR DIARY or INTELLIGENCE SUMMARY

Army Form C. 2118.

4010 75 Machine Gun Coy

Place	Date	Hour	Summary of Events and Information	Remarks and references to Appendices
LE BIZET	1-2-17		Enemy artillery and trench mortars particularly active. Indirect fire on following targets. Cross roads at B11 b.3.9. Bridges at C5a.3.3 and 3.5. Church square and main street, FRELINGHIEN. About 5.45 p.m. S.O.S. signal was observed on our left and barrage fire was opened immediately.	
"	2-2-17		Situation normal. Indirect fire on following targets. Suspected T.M. emplacement at C5a.0470. Cross roads at B11 b.3.9. Bridge at C11a.45.15.	
"	3-2-17		Situation normal. Weather very cold. All guns fired short bursts at intervals to prevent freezing. Following targets fired on. Bridges at C11a.45.15. C5a.3.3 and 3.5. Cross roads at B11 b.3.9.	
"	4-2-17		Situation quiet. Weather continued very cold so guns were fired at intervals as on 3rd. Following targets fired on. Cross roads at B11 b.3.9. Bridges at C5a.3.3 + 3.5. B11a.45.15. Enemy support line from CROWN PRINCE FARM to TWIN COTS. Church square, FRELINGHIEN.	
"	5-2-17		Situation very quiet. Weather very cold. Guns fired bursts as on last two days. Following targets fired on. Bridges at C5a.3.3., 3.5. B11a.45.15. Cross roads B11 b.3.9. FRELINGHIEN.	
"	6-2-17		Situation very quiet. Cold weather continues. Guns fired as before. Indirect fire on cross roads at B11 b.3.9. Bridges at C5a.3.3 + 3.5. Enemy support line from CROWN PRINCE FARM to TWIN COTS.	
"	7-2-17		Situation normal. Enemy trench mortars active. Guns fired bursts as on preceding days to prevent freezing. Following targets fired on. Enemy support line. Bridges at C5a.3.3.5. FRELINGHIEN	

Army Form C. 2118.

WAR DIARY
or
INTELLIGENCE SUMMARY.
(Erase heading not required.)

75 M.G. Coy

Place	Date	Hour	Summary of Events and Information	Remarks and references to Appendices
LE BIZET	8-2-17		Situation normal until 3 p.m. At 3 p.m. enemy artillery and trench mortars displayed great activity but by 4 p.m. situation was again normal. Following targets fired on. Cross roads at b.11.b.3.9. Bridges at b.5.a.3.3 and 3.5. b.11.a.45.15. Enemy support line from CROWN PRINCE FARM to TWIN COTS.	
"	9-2-17		Situation normal. Following targets fired on. Bridges at C.5.a.3.3 and 3.5. b.11.a.45.15. Cross roads at b.11.b.3.9. FRELINGHIEN. Church square.	
"	10-2-17		Enemy artillery and trench mortars active otherwise situation normal. Cold weather continued. Guns fired at intervals as before. Indirect fire on following targets. Cross roads at b.11.b.3.9. Bridges at C.5.a.3.3. 3.5 and C.11.a.45.15. Main St. FRELINGHIEN.	
"	11-2-17		Situation generally quiet but enemy trench mortars were active. Following targets fired on. Enemy support line from CROWN PRINCE FARM to TWIN COTS. Cross roads at b.11.b.3.9. Bridges at b.5.a.3.3, 3.5. C.11.a.45.15. Church square and main street. FRELINGHIEN.	
"	12-2-17		Situation normal. Following targets fired on. Bridges at b.5.a.3.3 and 3.5. b.11.a.45.15. Cross roads at b.11.b.3.9. Enemy support line from CROWN PRINCE FARM to TWIN COTS. Church square and main street. FRELINGHIEN. Road from C.11.b.35.90 to b.5 d.81.40.	

Army Form C. 2118.

WAR DIARY
or
INTELLIGENCE SUMMARY.
(Erase heading not required.)

75 M.G.C.

Instructions regarding War Diaries and Intelligence Summaries are contained in F. S. Regs., Part II. and the Staff Manual respectively. Title pages will be prepared in manuscript.

Place	Date	Hour	Summary of Events and Information	Remarks and references to Appendices
LE BIZET	13-2-17		Situation normal. Following targets fired on. Roads at b.11 b. 0.25. and b.5a 30.35. Bridge at PONT ROUGE U.29 b. 5.3 Enemy support line from CROWN PRINCE FARM to TWIN COTS. Bridges at b.5a 3.3, 3.5 and b.11 a 45.15. bivouacs at b.11 b 3.9. Church square FRELINGHIEN. Road from b.11 b 35.90 to b 5d 81.40.	
"	14-2-17		Situation normal. Indirect fire on PONT ROUGE (Bridge at U.29 b. 5.3). Enemy support line from CROWN PRINCE FARM to TWIN COTS. Bridges at b.5a 3.3, 3.5 and b.11 a 45.15. bivouacs at b.11 b 3.9. Road from C.11 b 35.90 to b.5 d 81.40.	
"	15-2-17		Situation normal. Indirect fire on enemy support line from CROWN PRINCE F.M to TWIN COTS. Bridges at U.29 b. 5.3 b.5a 3.3, 3.5 b.11 a 45.15 bivouacs at b.11 b.3.9. Church square FRELINGHIEN.	
"	16-2-17		Situation generally quiet. Following targets fired on. Enemy support line from CROWN PRINCE F.M to TWIN COTS. Bridges at U.29 b-5.3 b.5a 3.3, 3.5, b.11 a 45.15 Main St FRELINGHIEN. Enemy artillery and trench mortars active. Following targets fired on. Church square and main street	
"	17-2-17		FRELINGHIEN, Bridges at C.11 a 45.15. b.5a 3.3 and 3.5. U.29 b. 5.3 bivouacs at b.11 b. 3.9. Enemy support line from CROWN PRINCE FARM to TWIN COTS.	
"	18-2-17		Enemy machine guns active. LT J.L.H. FRASER severely wounded. This officer subsequently died from wounds. Indirect fire on targets as on 17th. We also fired on targets indicated by 75 Brigade in connection with raid on enemy trenches by 8th Bn South Lancs Regt.	

Army Form C. 2118.

WAR DIARY
or
INTELLIGENCE SUMMARY.
(Erase heading not required.)

7S M.G.Coy

Place	Date	Hour	Summary of Events and Information	Remarks and references to Appendices
Le Bizet	19-2-17		Situation normal. Following targets fired on. Bridge at U.29.b.5.3. b.5.a.3.3. and 3.5. b.11.a.45.15. Crossroads at b.11.b.3.9. Church Square and main street FRELINGHIEN.	
	20-2-17		Situation quiet. We fired on crossroads at b.11.b.3.9. Bridge at b.5.a.3.3. 3.5. b.11.a.45.15. U.29.b.5.3. FRELINGHIEN.	
	21-2-17		Situation normal. We fired on DURIEZ Fm and adjoining roads C.5.d.2.9. Crossroads b.11.b.3.9. Bridge at U.29.b.5.3. FRELINGHIEN.	
	22-2-17		Situation quiet. Following points fired on:- Bridges at U.29.b.5.3. b.5.a.3.3.3.5. b.11.a.45.15. Enemy support line from CROWN PRINCE FARM to TWIN COTS. Crossroads at C.11.b.3.9.	
	23-2-17		Enemy machine guns active. Otherwise situation quiet. We fired on enemy support line from CROWN PRINCE FARM to TWIN COTS. Crossroads at C.11.b.3.9. Bridge at C.5.a.3.3.,3.5. b.11.a.45.15.	
	24-2-17		Instructions received from G.O.C. 7S Infantry Brigade that Coy would be relieved in the line on Feb 25-17 by 1st New Zealand M.G.Coy. Details of relief to be arranged between O.C's concerned. Arrangements for relief were made in accordance with these instructions. Situation generally quiet but enemy machine guns displayed more than usual activity. We carried out indirect fire on the following targets:- Crossroads at b.11.b.3.9. Church square and main street, FRELINGHIEN. PONT ROUGE. Bridges at U.29.b.5.3. b.5.a.3.3. and 3.5. C.11.a.45.15.	

Army Form C. 2118.

WAR DIARY
or
INTELLIGENCE SUMMARY.

(Erase heading not required.)

75 M.G. Coy

Place	Date	Hour	Summary of Events and Information	Remarks and references to Appendices
Le Bizet	25-2-17		Company relieved by 1st New Zealand Machine Gun Coy as per arrangements made on 24th.	
		3.30p	Coy 1 left Le Bizet.	
Romarin		4.45p	Coy 1 arrived Romarin. HQ established at Vickers Camp.	
"	26-2-17	9.30a	Coy 2 left Romarin and marched via Bailleul, Meteren, Fletre and Caestre to Eecke Area. HQ established at Billet 6, Sheet 27, P.24.a.2.3.	
Eecke Area	27-2-17		Checking and repacking contents of limbers. Cleaning equipment and general routine work. Programme of training and classes for signallers and rangefinders arranged.	
"	28-2-17		Physical training. Squad drill, mechanism and stoppages in morning. Kit inspection and sports in afternoon. Signallers and rangefinders under instruction.	

No. 75 MACHINE GUN COMPANY
No. 1984
Date. 1-4-17

From O.C.
   75 Machine Gun Coʸ

To H.Q.
   75 Brigade.

Herewith please find Original War Diary for month of March 1917.

T. Shank   Captain,
Commanding
75 MACHINE GUN COY

Army Form C. 2118.

75 machine gun co
Vol XI

WAR DIARY
or
INTELLIGENCE SUMMARY
(Erase heading not required.)

Instructions regarding War Diaries and Intelligence Summaries are contained in F. S. Regs., Part II. and the Staff Manual respectively. Title Pages will be prepared in manuscript.

Place	Date	Hour	Summary of Events and Information	Remarks and references to Appendices
EECKE AREA	1-3-17		Company Training. Signallers and range finders under instructors	
"	2-3-17		Company Training. Signallers and range finders under instructors	
"	3-3-17		Company Training in morning. Route march in afternoon. Signallers and Rangefinders under instructors	
"	4-3-17		Co. attended gas demonstration by 25 Divisional gas officer in morning and sections fired on BEAUVOORDE and BERTENACRE ranges in afternoon. Divine service in evening.	
"	5-3-17		Company training and drill with limbers.	
"	6-3-17		Company training including advanced machine gun drill with limbers.	
"	7-3-17		Section on EECKE range in morning. Balance of Company training.	
"	8-3-17		Company training including approach to and attack on strong point. Range cards prepared and ground of advance reconnoitred for gun positions, limber concealment, establishment of dumps &c.	
"	9-3-17		Company took part with 75 Infantry Brigade in practice of advanced and rear guards.	
"	10-3-17		Section on EECKE range. Remainder of Company training.	

Army Form C. 2118.

WAR DIARY
or
INTELLIGENCE SUMMARY
(Erase heading not required.)

75 Machine Gun Coy

Place	Date	Hour	Summary of Events and Information	Remarks and references to Appendices
EECKE AREA	11-3-17		Divine service. Lectures by Section Officers.	
"	12-3-17		Instructions received that Coy would march to WEST RECOURT AREA commencing on 13th inst. Company engaged in packing limbers and cleaning equipment.	
"	13-3-17		Company left 9.0 a.m. and marched via HAZEBROUCK, EBBLINGHEM, & WALLON CAPPEL to WARDRECQUES.	
WARDRECQUES	14-3-17		Company left 9.30 a.m. and marched via ARQUES, WIZERNES & LUMBRES, to SENINGHEM.	
SENINGHEM	15-3-17		Company engaged in cleaning, checking and repacking contents of limbers and equipment.	
"	16-3-17		Company Training and machine gun drill.	
"	17-3-17		Company Training and machine gun drill.	
"	18-3-17		Company operations around village of SENINGHEM. 2 Sections attacking and 2 Sections defending.	
"	19-3-17		Instructions received from G.O.C. 75 Infantry Brigade that Coy would move to BORRE AREA. March to commence 20th. Limbers repacked and contents cleaned.	
"	20-3-17		Coy left 9.45 a.m. and marched via LUMBRES, SETQUES & ETREHEM to CORMETTE.	
CORMETTE	21-3-17		Coy left 8.0 a.m. and marched via ETREHEM, WISQUES, WIZERNES, ARQUES to RENESCURE.	
RENESCURE	22-3-17		Coy left 10.0 a.m. and marched via EBBLINGHEM, WALLON CAPPEL, HAZEBROUCK, and BORRE to SWARTENBROUCK.	
SWARTENBROUCK	23-3-17		Coy cleaning contents of limbers and equipment.	

Army Form C. 2118.

WAR DIARY
or
INTELLIGENCE SUMMARY

(Erase heading not required.)

75 Machine Gun Co¹

Place	Date	Hour	Summary of Events and Information	Remarks and references to Appendices
SWARTENBROUCK	24-3-17		Co¹ left 10.0 a.m. and marched via VIEUX BERQUIN to BLEU TOUR.	
BLEU TOUR	25-3-17		Co¹ cleaning contents of limbers and equipment. Divine service in afternoon.	
"	26-3-17		Co¹ training	
"	27-3-17		Section attached to 11 Bn Cheshire Regt. Remainder of Company training	
"	28-3-17		Company engaged on route march during morning. Training in afternoon.	
"	29-3-17		Section attached to 2 Bn South Lancs Regt. Remainder of Company training	
"	30-3-17		Section attached to 8 Bn South Lancs Regt. Remainder of Company training	
"	31-3-17		Section attached to 8 Bn Border Regt. Remainder of Company training.	

Army Form C. 2118.

75 Machine Gun Coy

Vol 12

WAR DIARY
or
INTELLIGENCE SUMMARY.
(Erase heading not required.)

Place	Date	Hour	Summary of Events and Information	Remarks and references to Appendices
BLEU TOUR	1-4-17		Company Training. Divine Service.	
"	2-4-17		Physical Training. Company training and Bombing instruction.	
"	3-4-17		Instructions received from G.O.C. 75 Infantry Brigade that 2 sections of this Coy would relieve sections of 3rd New Zealand Machine Gun Coy in the WULVERGHEM sector on April 4th. Officers & Sections of this Coy were to remain at BLEU TOUR until April 5. Captain T.E.Craik proceeded to H.Q. of the 3rd New Zealand Machine Gun Coy and arranged details of relief	
"	4-4-17		Nos 1 and 4 Sections of this Coy proceeded to BULFORD CAMP, NEUVE EGLISE and relieved 3rd New Zealand Machine Gun Coy	
"	5-4-17		Nos 2 & 3 Sections of this Coy left BLEU TOUR and marched via OUTTERSTEEN and BAILLEUL to BULFORD CAMP, NEUVE EGLISE. Sections in line reported generally quiet day	
NEUVE EGLISE	6-4-17		Enemy shelled positions at MIDLAND FARM but no damage resulted. Enemy Machine guns were active during night. We fired on MESSINES and WULVERGHEM - WYTSCHAETE Rd.	
"	7-4-17		Apart from some activity of enemy machine guns situation quiet. Our guns fired on enemy strong point at O.25.b.1.8 and as yesterday. Refs Sheet 28 SW 1:20000	
"	8-4-17		Reserve actions. Divine Service. Situation in line generally quiet except for occasional bursts from enemy machine guns. In addition to usual targets we fired on HELL FARM O.31.b.4.5. Sheet 28 SW 1:20000 2nd Anzac O.C. attended conference of machine gun Officers at Corps H.Q.	

Army Form C. 2118.

WAR DIARY
or
INTELLIGENCE SUMMARY.
(Erase heading not required.)

75 Machine Gun Coy

Instructions regarding War Diaries and Intelligence Summaries are contained in F. S. Regs., Part II. and the Staff Manual respectively. Title pages will be prepared in manuscript.

Place	Date	Hour	Summary of Events and Information	Remarks and references to Appendices
NEUVE EGLISE	9.4.17		Teams in line were relieved by teams in reserve. Usual targets were fired on by our guns. Situation generally quiet except for occasional shelling of Nord & S MIDLAND FARMS.	
	10.4.17		Enemy machine guns moderately active. No fired on usual targets.	
	11.4.17		Instructions received that this Coy would be relieved by the 74th Machine Gun Coy on 12th and that this Coy would proceed to the LA CRECHE Area. Arrangements for relief were though made with relieving Coy.	
	12.4.17		Coy relieved. Coy left 6.30pm and marched to STEEN-JE.	
STEEN-JE	13.4.17		General cleaning up.	
	14.4.17		Physical training, section drill and company drill. Bombing instruction and range practice. Working party of 1 O and 85 O R. provided for water work at LE VEAU. Balance of Coy training.	
	15.4.17		Working party provided as on 15th. Balance of Coy training. Bombing instruction and range practice.	
	16.4.17		Working party provided as on 16th, also party of 1 O O R. sent to PONT D'ACHELLES for work under ORDNANCE officer. Balance of Coy training. Bombing instruction and range practice.	
	17.4.17		Working parties provided as on 17th. Instructions received that this Coy was to relieve 7 Machine Gun Coy in the LE TOUQUET sector on 19th. Details of relief to be arranged between O.o. Coys.	
	18.4.17		Companies concerned.	

Army Form C. 2118.

WAR DIARY
or
INTELLIGENCE SUMMARY.
(Erase heading not required.)

Instructions regarding War Diaries and Intelligence Summaries are contained in F.S. Regs., Part II. and the Staff Manual respectively. Title pages will be prepared in manuscript.

75 Machine Gun Co.

Place	Date	Hour	Summary of Events and Information	Remarks and references to Appendices
STEEN-JE	19.4.17	8.30am	Co. left and marched via NIEPPE & PONT D'NIEPPE to LE BIZET. Relief of 7 Machine Gun Coy completed and Co. H.Q. established at LE BIZET.	
LE BIZET	20.4.17		RESERVE FARM shelled heavily. Our guns fired on LOOPHOLE FARM and UMPIRE DRIVE N-S. Refer PLOEGSTEERT Sheet 1-10000 U22d, 93 c and a. LIEUT T.C. BENNETT wounded.	
"	21.4.17		Situation normal, but enemy machine guns were active. Our guns fired on UMPIRE DRIVE N-S and UMPIRE ALLEY U22d 93 c.a. and 28 b. 29 a. Refer sheet as yesterday.	
"	22.4.17		Situation normal. Our guns fired on CELIA LANE Refer HOUPLINES Sheet 1-10000 C11 c and d. also on targets as yesterday.	
"	23.4.17		Enemy artillery and trench mortars active. Our guns fired on DURIEZ FM. Refer HOUPLINES sheet 1-10000 C5a	
"	24.4.17		Enemy shelled vicinity of LAWRENCE FM and LANCASHIRE SUPPORT FM. Our guns fired on DURIEZ FM as yesterday and on CELIA LANE as on 22nd.	
"	25.4.17		Enemy shelled vicinity of GUNNERS FM. Our guns fired at intervals on DURIEZ FM and CELIA LANE.	
"	26.4.17		Situation normal. Fired on FRELINGHIEN, DURIEZ FM. Bridges over river Lis at C11, e, 5, 9. Crossroads at C11 & 3.9. Refer HOUPLINES Sheet 1-10000	
"	27.4.17		Situation quiet. Indirect fire was carried out on targets as on 26th.	

Army Form C. 2118.

WAR DIARY
or
INTELLIGENCE SUMMARY.
(Erase heading not required.)

75 Machine Gun Co⁷

Place	Date	Hour	Summary of Events and Information	Remarks and references to Appendices
LE BIZET	28-4-17		Information received from G.O.C 75 Infantry Brigade that Co⁷ would be relieved on 29th by 9 Australian Machine Gun Co⁷. Arrangements made with O.C. that Co⁷ for relief. Enemy machine guns active, otherwise situation quiet.	
	29-4-17		At 12.30 a.m. 500 rounds discharged on Brigade front and surplus fired on FREUNDIEN BRIDGE, CECILIA RESERVE and BRICKFIELD, CECIL RESERVE, UNA SUPPORT, UMPIRE RESERVE and LOOPHOLE F9. Rifle HOUPLINES Sheet 1-10000. Co⁷ left LE BIZET at 11.30 a.m and marched via PONT DE NIEPPE to ERQUINGHEM - LYS.	
ERQUINGHEM - LYS	30-4-17		Co⁷ left at 1.30 p.m and marched to BLEU TOUR via SAILLY SUR LA LYS and LE VERRIER. Weather very hot and roads very dusty.	

From O.C.
　　75 Machine Gun Coy

To H.Q.
　　75 Brigade

No. 75
MACHINE GUN
COMPANY.

No. ....
Date. 1-5-17

Herewith please find original War diary for month of May 1917

_____ Captain,
Commanding
75 MACHINE GUN COY

Army Form C. 2118.

WAR DIARY
or
INTELLIGENCE SUMMARY.
(Erase heading not required.)

Instructions regarding War Diaries and Intelligence Summaries are contained in F. S. Regs., Part II. and the Staff Manual respectively. Title pages will be prepared in manuscript.

75 Machine Gun Co⁷

Vol 13

Place	Date	Hour	Summary of Events and Information	Remarks and references to Appendices
BLEU TOUR	1-5-17		Company training. O.C. attended conference at 75 Infantry Brigade HQ OUTTERSTEENE.	
	2-5-17		Company training.	
	3-5-17		Company training.	
	4-5-17		Company training.	
	5-5-17		Company training.	
	6-5-17		Company training.	
	7-5-17		Company training.	
	8-5-17		Company training.	
	9-5-17		Company training. Information received from G.O.C. 75 Infantry Brigade that Co⁷ would move into STEENT-JE area on 10th.	
	10-5-17	3pm	Company left	
STEENT-JE	"	5pm	Company arrived.	
"	11-5-17		Company training	
"	12-5-17		Company training	
"	13-5-17		Company training	
"	14-5-17		Instructions received from G.O.C. 75 Infantry Brigade that Co⁷ would move into LACRECHE area on 15th.	

Army Form C. 2118.

WAR DIARY
or
INTELLIGENCE SUMMARY.
(Erase heading not required.)

Instructions regarding War Diaries and Intelligence Summaries are contained in F. S. Regs., Part II. and the Staff Manual respectively. Title pages will be prepared in manuscript.

75 Machine Gun Coy

Place	Date	Hour	Summary of Events and Information	Remarks and references to Appendices
LA CRECHE	15-5-17		Coy moved from Steentje Area. Coy HQ at A.4.a.0.5 Sheet 36	
	16-5-17		Company training	
	17-5-17		Company training	
	18-5-17		Company training	
	19-5-17		Company training	
	20-5-17		Company training	
	21-5-17		Company training	
	22-5-17		Company training	
	23-5-17		Company training	
	24-5-17		Company training	
	25-5-17		Company training	
	26-5-17		Company training	
	27-5-17		Company training	
	28-5-17		Company training	
	29-5-17		Company moved to Ravelsberg area S.17.a.5.3 Sheet 28.	
RAVELSBURG	30-5-17		Company training	
	31-5-17		Company training	

From O/c 75 M.G.Co   **No. 75 MACHINE GUN COMPANY.**
                                        No. 2825
                                        Date 2-7-17

To H.Q.
      75 Brigade.

Herewith please find original War Diary for month of June 1917

                                 [signature] Lieut.
                                        O/c
                                             75 M.G.Co

Army Form C. 2118.

WAR DIARY
or
INTELLIGENCE SUMMARY.
(Erase heading not required.)

75 Machine Gun Coy.

Vol / 4

Place	Date	Hour	Summary of Events and Information	Remarks and references to Appendices
RAVELSBURG	1-6-17		Coy training	
	2-6-17		Coy training, checking, cleaning and packing limbers. Preparations made for active operations. The training on which the Coy had been engaged was for offensive operations and comprised :- Attack, defence of strong points with and without Infantry assistance. I Brigade and half Brigade schemes in which section of machine guns was allotted to each infantry battalion. III Advanced and rearguards.	
	3-6-17		No 2 section under 2 Lt AXH Some left camp at 9am and relieved 4 guns of 7 M.G.Cy at FORT PINKIE and 2 in WULVERGHEM SWITCH. Other 3 Sections moved at 7am and went into camp at T1c central (Sheet 28 S.W.) Guns in line fired on OCTOBER TRENCH O36c33a and STEENBECK valley in conjunction with operations carried out by artillery. Enemy shelled vicinity of WULVERGHEM switch.	
	4-6-17		Enemy shelling around gun positions in line nearly all day. One gun fired on track O31c 73·20 – 1570 during day also on STEENBECK (O31c), railway on road at O31 central - a97 during night on OCTOBER TRENCH (O32a). Sections in reserve continued training and general routine work.	
	5-6-17		Enemy shelled vicinity of FT PINKIE, SOUVENIR FM and WULVERGHEM SWITCH. Following targets were fired on. railway on road O31 central – a97. ground between SLOPING ROE FARM and O32d 85. Railway O31c 04, O31 central railway on road O31 central. O31d 45·30. BIRTHDAY FM. O32c 1445 – O32c 4055. STEENBECK. OZONE ALLEY. O31d 45·30.	

T2134. Wt. W708—776. 500000. 4/15. Sir J. C. & B.

Army Form C. 2118.

WAR DIARY
or
INTELLIGENCE SUMMARY.
(Erase heading not required.)

75 Machine Gun Coy

Place	Date	Hour	Summary of Events and Information	Remarks and references to Appendices
Ti C central	6.6.17		No. 4 Section and half No. 3 Section left to commence barrage work. Lt N.P. Bailey in command. No. 2 Section relieved. Barrage prepared for co-operation with Artillery & Infantry. Zero hour fixed for 3.10am - 7 June. Evening of 6th Coy was distributed and in position as follows: No. 1 Section under Lt C.W. Curry and Lt Pountney were attached to 8 Shrops. No. 2 Section under 2Lt A.W.H. Sime were in reserve at Coy H.Q. Forbes Terrace. Half No. 3 Section under 2 Lt Harkes with 11 Cheshires, half No. 3 Section and No. 4 Section under Lt N.P. Bailey were engaged in Barrage.	Refer Sheet 28 SW
	7.6.17		Attack scheduled for 3.10am was successful. The 4 guns with 8 Shrops and 2 guns with 11 Cheshires were pushed forward with battalions to which they were attached and consolidated positions in front of final objective of 75 Brigade. No. 2 section under 2 Lt A.W.H. Sime moved forward at 6am and formed line of protecting positions in line of posts established in front of objective. No. 4 Section and half No. 3 Section moved forward from barrage positions and took up fresh defensive positions in O.31.a. These positions covered front then held by 75 Brigade. Casualties - Lt P. Pountney killed, 2 Lt Harkes wounded. Coy H.Q. were moved forward to O.31.a. Captain T.E. Craik reconnoitred line and selected alternative positions.	

T2134. Wt. W708—776. 500000. 4/15. Sir J. C. & S.

Army Form C. 2118.

WAR DIARY
or
INTELLIGENCE SUMMARY.
(Erase heading not required.)

75 M.G.C.^y

Place	Date	Hour	Summary of Events and Information	Remarks and references to Appendices
Sheet 28 SW				
O31A	7.6.17	(cm)	2 Lt HARKES reported that on arrival at objective (at about 10.15a~) about 3 teams of 4 horses each, galloped down road half left from position he had taken up (in advance of the approximate position of N° 19 post) at a range of 1100 yards and after making certain that they were hostile artillery teams he opened fire. The teams and drivers took cover (or had reached their position) behind a thick hedge running south from the road. Fire was opened and hedge searched from top to bottom. Shortly afterwards (how and when galloped back along road, remainder did not appear. Heavy counter attack on the newly captured position took place on evening of 7th but this was beaten off. Our forward guns were put with good effect.	
"	8.6.17		Enemy artillery was very active. Guns were moved into fresh positions giving better field of fire.	
"	9.6.17		Enemy artillery again displayed great activity. Co^y was relieved by 7 M.G.C^y (with exception of N°1 Section and half N°3 section) and returned to camp at NEUVE EGLISE.	
"	10.6.17		N°4 section and half N°3 section moved forward and took up positions at O26d.15.35. SOS lines were laid and defensive positions arranged. Remainder of Co^y in camp at NEUVE EGLISE.	

Army Form C. 2118.

WAR DIARY
or
INTELLIGENCE SUMMARY

(Erase heading not required.)

75 M.G. Coy

Instructions regarding War Diaries and Intelligence Summaries are contained in F. S. Regs., Part II. and the Staff Manual respectively. Title Pages will be prepared in manuscript.

Place	Date	Hour	Summary of Events and Information	Remarks and references to Appendices
	11-6-17		Guns in defensive positions carried out some indirect fire on enemy positions. Enemy artillery very active.	
	12-6-17		No.4 section and half No.3 section were withdrawn and returned to camp at NEUVE EGLISE	
	13-6-17		Instructions received from G.O.C 75 Brigade that Coy would relieve 4th Australian M.G.Coy in the line 4 guns No.1 Section, 3 Teams No.2 Section, 1 Team No.3 Section accordingly left camp at NEUVE EGLISE. Balance of Coy with HQ moved to ONE SHELL FARM.	
	14-6-17		Arrangements made for attack of our enemy trench and establishing line of strong points between F.M DE LA CROIX – Building N/ GAPPARD. DECONIN F.M. CAPT G.S. DUCKWORTH with 2 guns and 2/Lt S.J. CURTIS were attached to attacking infantry. Zero was fixed for 7.30 p.m. Attack successful. Our guns were moved forward, positions were selected and consolidated.	
	15-6-17		New positions in advanced line were heavily shelled and guns were moved into alternative positions. Hostile patrols were engaged by our forward guns with good results.	
	16-6-17		Enemy shelled our positions heavily. Enemy aeroplanes were also active, descending to low level over our front line positions and firing with machine guns.	
	17-6-17		In view of continued heavy shelling, new positions were selected and guns moved. Enemy aeroplanes again displayed great activity	

Army Form C. 2118.

75 M.G.C.

WAR DIARY
or
INTELLIGENCE SUMMARY

(Erase heading not required.)

Place	Date	Hour	Summary of Events and Information	Remarks and references to Appendices
Tic central	18-6-17		Coo. 1 relieved by 74 M.G.C.s and moved into camp at Tic central	Sheet 2 PSW 1.2.0000
	19-6-17		Coo. 1 checking and cleaning equipment	
	20-6-17		Coo. 1 training	
	21-6-17		Coo. 1 training	
	22-6-17		Coo. 1 training	
	23-6-17		Coo. 1 left camp and marched to LA MOTTE	
LA MOTTE	24-6-17		Coo. 1 left, marched to MERVILLE	
MERVILLE	25-6-17		Coo. 1 left, marched to LESPESSES	
LESPESSES	26-6-17		Coo. 1 left, marched to PETIGNY	
PETIGNY	27-6-17		Coo. 1 training	
	28-6-17		Coo. 1 training	
	29-6-17		Coo. 1 training	
	30-6-17		Coo. 1 training	

From O.C.
    75 Machine Gun Coy

To H.Q.
    75 Brigade

    Herewith please find original war diary completed to end of July

6/8

T. Shanks Capt
O.C.
75 M.G.Coy

Army Form C. 2118.

WAR DIARY
or
INTELLIGENCE SUMMARY
(Erase heading not required.)

75 Machine Gun Co^y

Place	Date	Hour	Summary of Events and Information	Remarks and references to Appendices
PETIGNY	1-7-17		Company Training	
"	2-7-17		Company Training	
"	3-7-17		Company Training	
"	4-7-17		Company Training	
"	5-7-17		Company Training	
"	6-7-17		Company Training	
"	7-7-17		Instructions received from G.O.C. 75 Infantry Brigade that Co^y would move to VLAMERTINGHE area in two stages, on the 8 and 9 of July, the dismounted portion of the Co^y being moved by bus.	
"	8-7-17	8.0am	Co^y left PETIGNY, marched to BOMY, thence proceeded by motor bus to BOESEGHEM and marched from there to TANNAY.	
TANNAY	9-7-17	8.15am	Co^y left TANNAY, marched to HAZEBROUCK R^d thence proceeded by motor bus to a point about ½ mile SW of POPERINGHE, and marched from there to HALIFAX CAMP. H14c Sheet 28. 1-40000.	
HALIFAX CAMP	10-7-17		Co^y provided working party, consisting of 1 Officer and 35 OR's for work on new trench and construction of machine gun emplacements. Map reference of trench I 11 central. Sheet 28. Work on trench could only be carried out at night, and, owing to the enemy using exhaustatory shells, progress was slow. Balance of Co^y Training.	

2449 Wt. W14957/M90 750,000 1/16 J.B.C. & A. Forms/C.2118/12.

Army Form C. 2118.

WAR DIARY
or
INTELLIGENCE SUMMARY
(Erase heading not required.)

75 Machine Gun Coy

WO-95/

Place	Date	Hour	Summary of Events and Information	Remarks and references to Appendices
HALIFAX CAMP	11-7-17		Work on new trench and emplacements continued. Remainder of Coy training	
"	12-7-17		Work on new trench and emplacements continued. Remainder of Coy training.	
"	13-7-17		Work on new trench and emplacements continued. Remainder of Coy training.	
"	14-7-17		Work on new trench and emplacements continued. Remainder of Coy training.	
"	15-7-17		Work on new trench and emplacements continued. Remainder of Coy training.	
"	16-7-17		Work on new trench and emplacements continued. Remainder of Coy training.	
"	17-7-17		Work on new trench and emplacements continued. Remainder of Coy training.	
"	18-7-17		Work on new trench and emplacements continued. Remainder of Coy training.	
"	19-7-17		4 guns and teams under command of Captain G.S. Duckworth and 2LT T.C.C. Stanfield left and took up position in new trench & II central, to assist in carrying out a scheme of harassing fire on enemy trenches and tracks. Balance of Coy remained at HALIFAX CAMP	
"	20-7-17		Harassing fire continued. Balance of Coy training.	
"	21-7-17		Harassing fire continued. Balance of Coy training.	

Army Form C. 2118.

WAR DIARY
or
INTELLIGENCE SUMMARY
(Erase heading not required.)

75 Machine gun Co

Place	Date	Hour	Summary of Events and Information	Remarks and references to Appendices
HALIFAX CAMP	22-7-17		Harassing fire continued. Balance of Coy left HALIFAX CAMP at 9.30 pm and marched to LORNA CAMP. S of POPERINGHE.	
LORNA CAMP	23-7-17		Guns under Capt G.S. DUCKWORTH and Lt C.C. STANFIELD returned to camp.	
"	24-7-17			
"	25-7-17		Coy training	
"	26-7-17			
"	27-7-17			
"	28-7-17		Teams prepared, guns & equipment cleaned ready for active operations	
"	29-7-17		8 Barrage guns under Capt G.S. DUCKWORTH & 2Lt S.J. CURTIS left 4pm to assist in barrage on enemy trenches in connection with attack to be made on 31.05	
"	30-7-17		Coy left LORNA CAMP and marched to BELGIAN CHATEAU area	
BELGIAN CHATEAU AREA	31-7-17		Coy arrived 3am and left for Assembly position at 7.30 a.m. Arrived BECK TRENCH Iºe at 11 a.m.	

FROM O.C.
  75 MACHINE GUN COY.
TO
  H.Q.
    75 Brigade

No. 75
MACHINE GUN
COMPANY.
No. 2467
Date 31-8-17

Herewith please find War diary for month of August 1917.

T. Thain
Captain,
Commanding
75 MACHINE GUN COY

Army Form C. 2118.

WAR DIARY
or
INTELLIGENCE SUMMARY.
(Erase heading not required.)

75 Machine Gun Coy

Vol 16

Place	Date	Hour	Summary of Events and Information	Remarks and references to Appendices
BECK TRENCH	1-8-17		Instructions received from G.O.C. 75 Infantry Bde that this Coy would relieve the 23 Machine Gun Coy in the line, arrangements to be made between O's bdg Co's. Relief was carried out with great difficulty owing to the heavy nature of the ground and continued hostile shelling. Eventually guns were placed in positions as follows:- In front line at J.1.a.55.40. J.1.d.40.57. J.1.d.19 and J.1.a.92.10. About J.7.a.40.16. J.7.a.30.42. J.7.a.30.42. J.7.a.38.82. J.7.c.40.06. Reference sheets HOBRE 1-10000. Heavy rain all day	
	2-8-17		All gun positions and Coy. H.Q. heavily shelled. In forward positions no cover was available for men and guns and all trenches were flooded. 2 guns under 2LT ST CURTIS were placed in barrage positions at I.12.d.05.80 Sheet 28. Weather continued wet.	
	3-8-17		Rain practically all day. Enemy continued shelling all gun positions, both in front and support lines being shelled heavily. Hostile machine guns and snipers active	
	4-8-17		Enemy put down a heavy barrage in the vicinity of Zee House at 2.40 a.m. but no infantry action was reported. Weather continued wet until 4pm. From 5pm until dusk enemy aeroplanes flew over our lines, dropping smoke bombs and firing with machine guns at the troops manning our trenches. Usual heavy hostile shelling and machine gun activity	

Army Form C. 2118.

WAR DIARY
or
INTELLIGENCE SUMMARY
(Erase heading not required.)

75 Machine Gun Coy

Place	Date	Hour	Summary of Events and Information	Remarks and references to Appendices
BECK TRENCH	5-8-17		Weather dull and misty. Enemy counter attacked under cover of an extremely heavy barrage. Barrage guns fired on barrage lines. 6 more guns were placed in barrage positions at I.12.b.05.80. Sheet 28. By instructions of D.M.G.O remaining 8 teams were withdrawn and returned to PIONEER CAMP H.21.c. Sheet 28.	
PIONEER CAMP	6-8-17		Barrage guns reported heavy shelling of barrage positions	
"	7-8-17		Usual shelling and machine gun activity. About 9 pm S.O.S. was seen on left. All barrage guns fired on barrage lines from 9.5 pm to 9.35 pm by which time situation was normal. It was eventually established that this enemy counter attack was stopped by machine gun and artillery fire, the troops which had been assembled for the counter attack were practically annihilated and its few survivors fled in confusion. Enemy fired mustard oil shell around our barrage positions.	
"	8-8-17		Usual hostile shelling and activity by enemy machine guns and snipers	
"	9-8-17		Usual hostile shelling during day. During evening and night somewhat quieter.	

Army Form C. 2118.

WAR DIARY
or
INTELLIGENCE SUMMARY
(Erase heading not required.)

Instructions regarding War Diaries and Intelligence Summaries are contained in F. S. Regs., Part II. and the Staff Manual respectively. Title Pages will be prepared in manuscript.

Place	Date	Hour	Summary of Events and Information	Remarks and references to Appendices
PIONEER CAMP	10-8-17		At 4.35am allguns in barrage positions fired on barrage lines in support of an attack carried out by 74 Infantry Brigade. This attack was successful. Instructions received from G.O.C. 75 Infantry Brigade that Brigade would move to STEENVOORDE west area on morning of 12th.	75 machine gun Co[y]
	11-8-17		Instructions as to move on 12th cancelled and instructions received that 75 Brigade would relieve 74 Brigade in the line during night 11/12. 4 teams under 2Lt T.C.C. STANFIELD left to take up position in reserve at BECK TRENCH.	
	12-8-17		Instructions received from D.M.G.O. that 8 barrage guns of this Co[y] would be relieved by teams from 23rd Machine Gun Co[y] on 13th. Barrage positions shelled heavily.	
	13-8-17		Relief of barrage guns completed and teams returned to PIONEER CAMP. On instructions received from 25 Division 2 guns and teams under 2Lt S.J. CURTIS relieved 2 guns of 8th Division on anti aircraft duties at OUDERDOM ammunition dump.	
	14-8-17		4 teams under 2Lt T.C.C. STANFIELD returned from BECK TRENCH.	
	15-8-17		Co[y] checking and cleaning equipment and refitting.	

Army Form C. 2118.

75 Machine Gun Co.

WAR DIARY
or
INTELLIGENCE SUMMARY
(Erase heading not required.)

Instructions regarding War Diaries and Intelligence Summaries are contained in F.S. Regs., Part II. and the Staff Manual respectively. Title Pages will be prepared in manuscript.

Place	Date	Hour	Summary of Events and Information	Remarks and references to Appendices
PIONEER CAMP	16-8-17		Co. checking and cleaning equipments. During night 16/17 hostile aeroplanes dropped bombs in back area. The A.A. guns of this Co. at OUDERDOM were fired at the raiding planes	
"	17-8-17		Instructions received from G.O.C. 75 Infantry Brigade that Brigade would move to EECKE area by bus on night 17/18. Transport moved by road to new area.	
EECKE	18-8-17		Co. arrived. A.A. guns at OUDERDOM fired on enemy aeroplanes who had dropped bombs in vicinity.	
"	19-8-17		Co. training. A.A. guns at OUDERDOM fired on enemy aeroplanes at night.	
"	20-8-17		Co. moved to farm at K.26.d.8.9. Sheet 27.	
STEENVOORDE	21-8-17		Co. training	
"	22-8-17		Co. marched to farm at J.15.a.7.7. Sheet 27.	
WINNEZEELE	23-8-17 to 31-8-17		Co. training	

FROM O.C.
75 MACHINE GUN COY.

TO H.Q.
    75 Brigade

> No. 75
> MACHINE GUN
> COMPANY
> No. 9577
> Date 9-10-17

Attached please find original War diary for October 1917.

P. Shank, Captain,
Commanding
75 MACHINE GUN COY.

Army Form C. 2118.

WAR DIARY
or
INTELLIGENCE SUMMARY
(Erase heading not required.)

Instructions regarding War Diaries and Intelligence Summaries are contained in F. S. Regs., Part II. and the Staff Manual respectively. Title Pages will be prepared in manuscript.

75 M.G. Coy

Vol 17

Place	Date	Hour	Summary of Events and Information	Remarks and references to Appendices
OUDEZEELE	1-9-17		Coy left at 12 noon, marched via STEENVOORDE, ABEELE and DICKEBUSCH to SCOTTISH CAMP	
DICKEBUSCH	2-9-17		Coy left SCOTTISH CAMP and marched to camp at H.97.b.6.5 Sheet 28.	
	3-9-17 5-9-17		Coy Training	
	5-9-17		Coy relieved 7 machine gun Coy in the line. Coy H.Q. being established at HALFWAY HOUSE. I.17.c. Sheet 28. Machine guns were placed at J.14.a.30.20, 35.25, 70.55, and 80.50 in the forward trenches and at J.13.b. 70.50, 75.45, 65.50, 60.40, 55.35, and 50.60 for barrage work. Enemy shelling was very heavy between 4.30 and 5.0 pm and great difficulty was experienced in getting guns into position. 10 OR killed and 30 OR wounded.	
HALFWAY HOUSE	6-9-17		Night 5/6 enemy continued active, particularly artillery and machine guns. Some gas shells were fired around barrage positions. Preparations made for barrage fire to commence night 6/7. About 7.30 pm enemy put down a heavy barrage on left of our positions and our guns fired on barrage lines in response to S.O.S. Guns also fired during night according to barrage programme.	
"	7-9-17.		Generally quiet day but enemy snipers displayed some activity. Enemy shelling became heavy during night, some gas shells being used. Barrage fire according to programme was carried out during night 7/8 and early morning. Hostile patrols were active during night 7/8.	

2449 Wt. W14957/Mgo 750,000 1/16 J.B.C. & A. Forms/C.2118/12.

Army Form C. 2118.

WAR DIARY
or
INTELLIGENCE SUMMARY
(Erase heading not required.)

75 M.G. Coy

Instructions regarding War Diaries and Intelligence Summaries are contained in F. S. Regs., Part II and the Staff Manual respectively. Title Pages will be prepared in manuscript.

Place	Date	Hour	Summary of Events and Information	Remarks and references to Appendices
HALFWAY HSE	8-9-17		Enemy artillery and snipers active. Information received that Coy would be relieved on 9th by 141 Machine Gun Boy. Barrage fire carried out during night 8/9 as per programme. Enemy shelling particularly heavy in vicinity of barrage positions.	
	9-9-17		Enemy shelling continued during early morning. 5 O.R. killed 3 O.R. wounded. In accordance with arrangements made teams were relieved by teams from 141 M.G. Coy and Coy H.Q. were moved from HALFWAY HOUSE to camp at H.27.b.5. Sheet 28. No 15 of forward gun teams remained in line until early morning 10th.	
DICKEBUSCH	10-9-17		Boy. checking and cleaning guns and equipment. Marched to HALIFAX CAMP	
HALIFAX CAMP	11-9-17		Boy. cleaning equipment.	
	12-9-17		Boy. left Halifax Camp and moved by bus to CAESTRE.	
CAESTRE	13-9-17		Boy. left and marched via HAZEBROUCK, MORBECQUE, STEENBECQUE and THIENNES to TANNAY.	
TANNAY	14-9-17		Coy. marched via LAMBRES, NORRENT FONTES, LILLERS and LOZINGHEM to MARLES LES MINES	
MARLES LES MINES	15-9-17 – 26-9-17		Boy. training.	
	26-9-17		Instructions received from G.O.C. 75 Infantry Brigade that Boy would relieve 71 M.G. Coy in the line night 29/30. Details to be arranged between O.C. & Boy.	

WAR DIARY
or
INTELLIGENCE SUMMARY
(Erase heading not required.)

Army Form C. 2118.

75 M.G.C⁰ᶻ

Place	Date	Hour	Summary of Events and Information	Remarks and references to Appendices
MARLES LES MINES	27-9-17	9·0 AM	Coy. left. Marched to Noeux Les Mines.	
NOEUX LES MINES	28-9-17		Capt. T. E. CRAIK interviewed O.C. 71 M.G.C⁰ᶻ and arranged details of relief on night 29/30.	
	29-9-17	4·0 P	Coy. left. Marched to Cité St Pierre. At conclusion of relief of 71 M.G.C⁰ᶻ disposition of Coy. was as follows:- 2 sections in the line. Guns at M12c51, M18d 35.60, M12 & B.O. N7c14, N13 & 19., N13 & 5.8., N7d.9.0., N8c1.9., 1 section. 4 guns at Coᶻ HQ. M18a 4.5. Reference sheet LENS TRENCH MAP 1:10000. 1 section 4 guns at Transport lines PETIT SAINS.	
CITÉ ST PIERRE	30-9-17		During night 29/30 harrassing fire was carried out on enemy trenches roads and tracks. 5000 rounds S.A.A. expended. A.A. gun at CITÉ ST PIERRE fired on E.A. Situation normal	

Army Form C. 2118.

WAR DIARY
or
INTELLIGENCE SUMMARY.
(Erase heading not required.)

Vol 15   75 Machine Gun Co.

Place	Date	Hour	Summary of Events and Information	Remarks and references to Appendices
CITE ST PIERRE	1-10-17		Situation very quiet. Practically no activity on part of the enemy. We fired on Trench junction N.15.a 35.45 and on Church square, LENS N.21.a.1.9. Sheet 36c S.W. 1-20000	
"	2-10-17		Situation normal. We fired on Church square. LENS N.21.a.1.9 and on road N.14.d 8.5-8.7.	
"	3-10-17		Situation normal. Very little movement observed. We fired on Church square. LENS N.21.a.1.9 road N.14.d 8.5-8.7 road junction N.14.d 85.35. Instructions received that Bn would be relieved by 16 M.G.Coy night 5/6.	
"	4-10-17		Situation normal until evening when enemy artillery and trench mortars displayed considerable activity, especially on right of Brigade sector. We fired on Church square. LENS N.21.a.1.9. roads at N.14.d 8.5-8.7 road junction N.14.d 85.35.	
"	5-10-17		Situation normal and generally quiet. Bn was relieved by 16 M.G.Coy and marched to NOEUX LES MINES. Instructions received from 75 Brigade that Bn would relieve 5 M.G.Coy in the CANAL sector. Sheet 36c N.W. 1-20000. On Oct 6. Captain T.E. Crosle reconnoitred new line to be taken over and completed details of relief with O.C. 5 M.G.Co.	
NOEUX LES MINES	6-10-17		Company left at 10.0 a.m. marched to LE PREOL and relieved 5 M.G.Coy in the CANAL sector. Bn HQ at LE PREOL. F.15.b.7.4. Sheet 36b N.E. Bn placed before in the line. Situation very quiet.	
LE PREOL	7-10-17		Situation quiet. Indirect fire was carried out on enemy Battn HQ at A.29.d 35.90 at intervals during night.	

Army Form C. 2118.

WAR DIARY
or
INTELLIGENCE SUMMARY.
(Erase heading not required.)

75 Machine Gun Coy

Place	Date	Hour	Summary of Events and Information	Remarks and references to Appendices
LE PREOL	8-10-17		Enemy machine guns displayed some activity during night 7/8. We fired on CAMBRIN - LA BASSEE Rd between A.22.b.8.5 and A.23.b.8.9, also right railway and track from A.17.d.6.7 to A.18.b.3.8. Sheet 36c NW.	
	9-10-17		Some Enemy minenwerfer activity and also machine gun activity during night 8/9. Bursts were fired by us on LA BASSEE Rd between A.22.b.8.5 and A.23.b.8.9. Instructions received that Coy will be relieved by 195 M.G.Coy on 10th. Details of relief were arranged by Captain T.E. CRAIK with O.C. 195 M.G.Coy	
	10-10-17		Relief of Coy was carried out in accordance with arrangements made. After relief Coy marched to BEUVRY	
BEUVRY	11-10-17 – 19-10-17		Coy Training. Details of relief of 195 M.G.Coy in CANAL SECTOR was arranged in accordance with instructions issued by 25th Division. Relief to take place afternoon 20th.	
	20-10-17		Coy left noon, marched to LE PREOL and relieved 195 M.G.Coy in the CANAL Sector as arranged. Coys HQ established at LE PREOL F.15.b.74 Sheet 36c NE. Enemy artillery active around church at CUINCHY. We fired on X roads A.29.a.19 and on road A.29.a.b.3.00 - A.29.a.6.62. Sheet 36c NW	
LE PREOL	21-10-17		Situation normal. Enemy Machine guns active during night. We fired on enemy Field Kitchen at A.29.c.52.13 and Railway in A.22.b. Sheet 36c NW.	

WAR DIARY
or
INTELLIGENCE SUMMARY.

Army Form C. 2118.

(Erase heading not required.)

Instructions regarding War Diaries and Intelligence Summaries are contained in F. S. Regs., Part II. and the Staff Manual respectively. Title pages will be prepared in manuscript.

Place	Date	Hour	Summary of Events and Information	Remarks and references to Appendices
Le Preol	22-10-17		Situation normal. Harassing fire was carried out on railway in A.22.b. Road at A.16.5.5.5. Cross roads at A.23.c.15.45. Road at A.29.a.63.00 – A.29.c.t.6. Road A.29.b.24.00 – b.35.45	75 machine gun Coy. 1 O.R wounded
	23-10-17		Situation normal. The fired on enemy patrol near our wire Road A.29.b.24.00 – b.35.45 and A.16.b and Towpath at A.16.d. S.S. Enemy support lines in A.10.c and A.16.b.	
	24-10-17		Enemy shelled heavily and two machine guns and Trench mortars were also in action. Information having been received that an enemy raid on our line North of CANAL would probably be attempted night 24/25, two guns of this Bn with a enemy party of infantry, took up a position in No Mans Land at A.16.a.10.00 at 6pm. Usual harassing fire was carried out. Guns at A.16.a.10.00 were withdrawn at 3am. Enemy artillery active about 4.15am. Under cover of this bombardment the enemy raided our front line trenches near Finchley Rd. Harassing fire was carried out on Batln HQ at A.29.b.55.90 Towpath A.16.d.S.S and Railway A.16.d.9.1.	
	25-10-17		Situation normal. Enemy machine guns less active than on previous nights. Usual harassing fire was carried out on following targets. Battalment H.29.d.55.35. Towpath A.16.d.S.S. C.T. A.10.£.9.1.	
	26-10-17		Hostile artillery active especially around our front line and forward posture. Enemy machine guns also active. Following enemy positions fired on Railway system in A.22.b. Towpath in A.16.b. Support line in A.10.c.	

Army Form C. 2118.

WAR DIARY
or
INTELLIGENCE SUMMARY.

(Erase heading not required.)

75 Machine Gun Co²

Place	Date	Hour	Summary of Events and Information	Remarks and references to Appendices
LE PREOL	28-10-17		Situation normal. Usual enemy machine gun activity at night. Barronades A39a19. AUCHY, A23c. and Towpath A16d 5.5 fired on.	
	29-10-17		Situation normal. Following enemy positions fired on. Towpath A16d. AUCHY, A23c ROAD A23a 35 40. Farm A29a 25.00.	
	30-10-17		Situation normal. The pond on LONE FARM A29a 25.00. Towpath A16d S.S REG HQ A11c 9.4. In accordance with instructions issued by 25th Division, machine guns at A15a 48.74, A15a 60.55, A21c 86.76, A21d 87.82 were withdrawn and positions at A27a 97 were handed over to 74 M.G. Co². These guns were then placed in SUSSEX TRENCH at G.30.2.4. for S.O.S. purposes.	
	31-10-17		Situation normal. NCO i/c positions at A11bc 05 45 reported that a red rocket was sent up from enemy lines at about A22a37 at 5.50pm. A few seconds after gas was discharged by the enemy from this point. During night usual harassing fire was carried out on following targets Battalion HQ A29d 35.90 REG HQ A11c9.4 Barroadade Machine gun activity by enemy.	

Peter Mort, Captain.
Commanding
75 MACHINE GUN CO⁷

FROM O.C.
75 MACHINE GUN COY.

To H.Q.
　　　75 Brigade.

No. 75
MACHINE GUN
COMPANY
No. 2766
Date 2-12-17

　　　　　　　original
Herewith ~~duplicate~~ War Diary for
November 1917.

　　　　　　　　　　　　A Sharp　　Captain,
　　　　　　　　　　　Commanding
　　　　　　　　　　75 MACHINE GUN COY

WAR DIARY
or
INTELLIGENCE SUMMARY.

Army Form C. 2118.

Vol 19 — 75 machine gun bn.

Place	Date	Hour	Summary of Events and Information	Remarks and references to Appendices
LE PREOL			REFERENCE MAP LA BASSEÉ 36c NW 1. 1/10000	
	1-11-17		Situation during day normal. Following targets were fired on:- ROAD A29 b.24.00 - b.35.45 and b.00 Roads A11c 18.94.	
"	2-11-17		Between 10am and 4pm enemy displayed considerable activity immediately North of CANAL with Minenwerfers, H.V. and 5.9. Following targets were fired on during night. Dump at A23c 95.25 Cross Rds at A 11c 18.90.	
"	3-11-17		Situation normal with exception of Enemy machine guns which were exceptionally active. Following targets were fired on. DUMP A23a 41.10. REG H.Q. A11c 90.40.	
"	4-11-17		Situation quiet. Following targets were fired on CROSS Rds A11c 18.90 and CROSS Rds A29c 10.90.	
"	5-11-17		Situation quiet. We fired on CROSS Rds A 11c 18.90 and BATTN HQ. A 23 c.	
"	6-11-17		Situation normal. We fired on TRAMWAY A.23a 40.70 - A17c 80.15. and A.23c 52.13.	
"	7-11-17		Situation normal. We fired on REG H.Q. A11c 9.4. and AUCHY LEZ LA BASSEÉ A.23 c.	
"	8-11-17		Situation normal. Following targets fired on:- CROSS Rds A 11c 18.90 and A.23c 15.45	
"	9-11-17		Situation normal, with exception of Enemy M.G's. which were less active than usual. Following targets were fired on. DUMP A.23c.95.25. and CROSS Rd A11c 18.90.	

Army Form C. 2118.

WAR DIARY
or
INTELLIGENCE SUMMARY.
(Erase heading not required.)

Place	Date	Hour	Summary of Events and Information	Remarks and references to Appendices
LE PREOL.	10-11-17		Enemy artillery active between 12.30 and 1 p.m. Between 6 and 6.10 p.m. S.O.S signal was observed N of CANAL and our guns fired on S.O.S lines. Usual harassing fire was carried out on the following targets:- CROSS R^ds A.23 c 15.45. TRAMWAY A.23a 40.70 - A.17c 80.15.	75 machine gun Co"
	11-11-17		Situation during last 24 hours normal. Enemy artillery displayed some activity around our gun positions. Harassing fire was carried out on BATT^n H.Q. A.29.b 35.90 and REG. H.Q. A.11c 94.	
	12-11-17		Situation normal. We fired on CROSS R^ds A.29a 10.90 and TRAMWAY A.23a 40.70 - 17c 80.15.	
	13-11-17		Enemy T.M's very active in vicinity of BRICKSTACK'S otherwise situation normal. We fired on ROAD A.29 b. 35.45. TRAMWAY A.23 a 47 - A.17c 80.15	
	14-11-17		Information received from G.O.C 75 Brigade that an enemy raid was expected to take place on our lines N of the CANAL. A gun was placed in position at A.16c 10.55 to cover No Man's Land to NORTH. As nothing unusual occurred gun was withdrawn at 5.30 a.m. (15). We fired on ESTAMINET at A.29a 55.35.	
	15-11-17		Situation normal. We fired on A.23c 95.25. Gun was placed in position at A.16c 10.55 as on (14th) and withdrawn at daylight.	
	16-11-17		Situation normal. We fired on A.29a 10.90 and placed gun in position at A.16c 10.55 as on previous nights.	

Army Form C. 2118.

WAR DIARY
or
INTELLIGENCE SUMMARY.
(Erase heading not required.)

75 Machine Gun Co?

Place	Date	Hour	Summary of Events and Information	Remarks and references to Appendices
LE PREOL	17-11-17		Situation normal. Harassing fire was carried out on ROAD A29b 26.50 - 35.45. Gun was again placed in position at A16c 10.55 and withdrawn at daylight.	
"	18-11-17		Situation normal. Corons de PEKIN A29c was fired on by our guns during the day and the following targets at night AUCHY A23 a 20.40 - 29 b 10.90 ROAD A29 b 35.45 - 15.85. TOWPATH ALLEY. A17d 15.40 - 80.75.	
"	19-11-17		Situation normal. We fired on AUCHY. A23a 20.40 - 29 b 10.90	
"	20-11-17		Enemy artillery active between 3.30 - 4 pm apparently in retaliation for a bombardment from our artillery. CAMBRIN - LA BASSEE Rd A18c 40.40 - 80.60 was fired on during the day and CEMETERY TRENCH A19d 25.40 - 29 b 40.10 and TRENCH Jct at G 5 b 20.90 during night.	
"	21-11-17		Situation normal. Harassing fire was carried out on CORONS DE PEKIN A29c	
"	22-11-17		Situation normal, but enemy machine guns displayed more activity than usual during day. We fired on TOW PATH ALLEY A17d 15.40 - 80.75 and Field Kitchen A23 c 52 13.	
"	23-11-17		Enemy artillery active, the vicinity of COLDSTREAM LANE and our support line being shelled heavily. We fired on CROSS Rds A23c 15.45	
"	24-11-17		Situation normal. We fired on CROSS Rds A23c 15.45.	

Army Form C. 2118.

WAR DIARY
or
INTELLIGENCE SUMMARY.
(Erase heading not required.)

75 M G Coy

Place	Date	Hour	Summary of Events and Information	Remarks and references to Appendices
LE PREOL	25.11.17		Situation normal. We fired on LONE FARM A.29.a. 00.25 and LEFT S.O.S. lines during day and on AUCHY A.23.a. 20.40 - 29.b.10.90 and TOWPATH ALLEY A.16.d. 05.60 - 17.d. 15.40 during night. Remains of Coy taken over by Captain A.P. STRANGE	
	26.11.17		Situation normal. Following targets on enemy lines fired on TOWPATH ALLEY A.16.d. 05.60 - 17.d.15.40 and AUCHY A.23.a. 20.40 - 29.b.10.90.	
	27.11.17		Information received from 75 Infantry Brigade that Boi would be relieved on 29th and would march to BOMY area. We fired on DISTILLERY A.18.c. and TOWPATH ALLEY A.17.d. 15.40 - 80.75	
	28.11.17		Enemy machine guns more than usually active. We fired on CEMETERY TRENCH A.29.a. TRENCH JCTN G.S.A.20.90 CEMETERY TRENCH A.29.a. 25.40	
	29.11.17		Coy relieved by 12 S.M.G. Coy and marched to BURBURE.	
BURBURE	30.11.17		Coy left, marched to PETIGNY.	
PETIGNY	30.11.17		Coy arrived.	

Army Form C. 2118.

WAR DIARY
or
INTELLIGENCE SUMMARY.
(Erase heading not required.)

75 Machine Gun Coy

Vol 20

Place	Date	Hour	Summary of Events and Information	Remarks and references to Appendices
PETIGNY	1-12-17		Coy marched to VINCHY	
VINCHY	2-12-17		Instructions received from 75 Infantry Brigade that Brigade would move by rail on Dec 3 to Third Army Area. Preparations made for rail journey.	
"	3-12-17		Coy marched to ANVIN, entrained.	
ACHIET LE GRAND	4-12-17		Coy detrained and marched to camp at GOMIECOURT	
GOMIECOURT	5-12-17		Coy marched to ROCQUIGNY.	
ROCQUIGNY	6-12-17 / 8-12-17		Coy cleaning guns and equipment.	
"	9-12-17		Coy marched to BAPAUME.	
BAPAUME	10-12-17		Coy training.	
"	11-12-17	1.0 AM	Instructions received from 25 Division that Coy would report at H.Q. 75 Infantry Brigade at 6.30 a.m. Coy marched to FAVREUIL.	
FAVREUIL	12-12-17 / 20-12-17		Coy training	
"	21-12-17		Instructions received from 25 Division that Coy would relieve 7 M.G.Coy in the LAGNICOURT sector on 21st. Relief was carried out successfully.	

Army Form C. 2118.

WAR DIARY
or
INTELLIGENCE SUMMARY.
(Erase heading not required.)

Instructions regarding War Diaries and Intelligence Summaries are contained in F. S. Regs., Part II. and the Staff Manual respectively. Title pages will be prepared in manuscript.

75 M.G.C²

Place	Date	Hour	Summary of Events and Information	Remarks and references to Appendices
LAGNICOURT	22-12-17		Situation during day and night normal. Enemy machine guns slightly active. Our guns fired occasional bursts during night to prevent freezing.	
	23-12-17		Situation normal. Our guns fired occasional bursts on S.O.S lines to prevent freezing.	
	24-12-17		Situation normal. Our guns fired occasional bursts to prevent freezing.	
	25-12-17		Situation normal. On instructions received from 25 Division ten guns of 7 M.G.C⁰ʸ were placed in position to reinforce guns of this Co².	
	26-12-17		No change in situation which contained normal. Our guns fired occasional bursts on S.O.S lines. Situation unchanged.	
	27-12-17		Guns of 7 M.G.C⁰ʸ were withdrawn.	
	28-12-17		Situation unchanged. Occasional bursts were fired by our guns on S.O.S lines.	
	29-12-17		No change in situation. Occasional bursts were fired by our guns as previously.	
	30-12-17		Enemy shelled vicinity of LAGNICOURT, otherwise no change in situation.	
	31-12-17		On instructions received from 25 Division ten guns of 7 M.G.C⁰ʸ were placed in position to reinforce guns of this Co². Situation normal. Our guns fired short bursts on S.O.S lines during night.	

AShaw
Major
Commanding 75 M.G. Company.

WAR DIARY
or
INTELLIGENCE SUMMARY.
(Erase heading not required.)

Army Form C. 2118.

75 Machine Gun Co.

Place	Date	Hour	Summary of Events and Information	Remarks and references to Appendices
LAGNICOURT	1-1-18		Situation quiet and unchanged. During so cold guns fired short bursts on SOS line at intervals to prevent freezing.	
	2-1-18		Instructions received from 25 Division that Co. would be relieved night 2/3 Jany by 7 M.G. Co. Details of relief to be arranged between Co. Bdy. Co. Relief completed and Co. moved into Camp No. 5 FAYREUIL.	
FAYREUIL	3-1-18 / 9-1-18		Co. Training.	
"	10-1-18		Instructions received from 25 Division that Co. would move into the line night 10/11 Jany and take over from the 195 M.G. Co. from positions 5, 6, 7 & 8 also man C, D & E battery positions 4 guns each battery. Arrangements for relief made and relief carried out satisfactorily. Co. H.Q. at C.28.d.90.90 Sheet 57c 1:40000.	
"	11-1-18		Situation very quiet. Very little activity on the part of the enemy.	
"	12-1-18		Situation unchanged and generally quiet.	
"	13-1-18		No change in situation. Enemy activity slight. Our guns fired occasional bursts on S.O.S. lines.	

Army Form C. 2118.

WAR DIARY
or
INTELLIGENCE SUMMARY.
(Erase heading not required.)

75 Machine Gun Coy

Place	Date	Hour	Summary of Events and Information	Remarks and references to Appendices
LAGNICOURT	14-1-18		Situation quiet and unchanged.	
"	15-1-18		Situation quiet and unchanged.	
"	16-1-18		Instructions received from 25 Division that this Coy would relieve the 7 M.G. Coy in the left section on night 17/18 Jany, vacating C.D.& E battery positions. Arrangements made for relief as instructed. Situation in line quiet and unchanged.	
"	17-1-18		Relief of 7 M.G. Coy completed. Situation normal	
"	18-1-18		Situation unchanged. Instructions received from 25 Division that Coy would be relieved by the 19S. M.G. Coy evening of 19 Jany. Arrangements for relief completed	
"	19-1-18		Coy relieved by 19S M.G. Coy and moved to Camp 28 FAVREUIL.	
FAVREUIL	20-1-18 – 22-1-18		Coy Training, checking equipment &c.	
"	23-1-18	PM 11-0	Instructions received from 25 Division that D & E battery positions were to be manned. Guns to be in position and laid on left S.O.S lines by 6 a.m. 24 th. 2 Lt BENTLEY and 2 Lt SIME with 8 guns and teams left to man positions noted above.	

Army Form C. 2118.

WAR DIARY
or
INTELLIGENCE SUMMARY.
(Erase heading not required.)

75 Machine Gun Co.

Place	Date	Hour	Summary of Events and Information	Remarks and references to Appendices
FAVREUIL	24-1-18	3-0 PM	Instructions received from 25 Division to withdraw guns and teams from D & E batteries. Instructions carried out. Enemy shell exploded close to limber. 1 OR killed. 2 OR wounded.	
"	25-1-18		Instructions received from 35 Division that this Co. would move into the line night Jan 26 and occupy C, D, E battery positions, and take over from the 74 MGC. Arrangements for above completed.	
"	26-1-18		Guns 5.6.7.8. Co. moved into the line, relieved guns of 74 MGC at positions 5.6.7.8 and occupied C D E batteries. Co. HQ at B.28.b.90.90. Sheet 57c 1-40000. Enemy artillery more active than usual.	
LAGNICOURT	27-1-18		Apart from occasional shelling of LAGNICOURT village situation was very quiet.	
"	28-1-18		Situation quiet and unchanged. During night enemy machine guns were active firing on roads leading to LAGNICOURT.	
"	29-1-18		Situation normal. LAGNICOURT shelled at intervals during night.	
"	30-1-18		Situation very quiet. No enemy activity.	
"	31-1-18			

Major
75 M. G. Co.

From O.C.
    C Coy, 25 Battalion, M.G.C

To O.C.
    25 Battalion
        M.G.C.

Attached please find original War Diary for month of February 1918.

                  J. Duckworth Capt
                    for Major
                    Oly
                      C Coy

1-3-18

Army Form C. 2118.

WAR DIARY
or
INTELLIGENCE SUMMARY.
(Erase heading not required.)

75 Machine Gun Co.

Place	Date	Hour	Summary of Events and Information	Remarks and references to Appendices
LAGNICOURT	1-2-18		General situation quiet and unchanged. LAGNICOURT was shelled at intervals during night.	
"	2-2-18		General situation quiet and unchanged. Enemy Aircraft displayed some activity.	
"	3-2-18		LAGNICOURT was shelled at intervals otherwise situation remained quiet and unchanged	
"	4-2-18		Enemy quiet until evening, when artillery displayed some activity. Numerous coloured lights were fired by the enemy at 8 p.m. but no enemy action followed.	
"	5-2-18	5 a.m.	Our front lines were shelled by the enemy otherwise situation for the whole of the day was quiet and unchanged. LAGNICOURT was shelled at intervals during the night. Under instructions received from D.M.G.O. 'C' Battery was withdrawn, also 2 guns from 'D' & 'E' Batteries. These were placed on the Corps line of defence under 2 Lt R.W.Potts	
"	6-2-18		Situation quiet during the morning. Our Artillery bombarded enemy front line between 12-12.15 p.m. Enemy retaliated during the afternoon.	
"	7-2-18		Situation generally quiet and unchanged. Enemy artillery slightly active during the evening	
"	8-2-18		General situation quiet and unchanged. LAGNICOURT was shelled at intervals during the night.	

Army Form C. 2118.

WAR DIARY
or
INTELLIGENCE SUMMARY.
(Erase heading not required.)

75 M.G. Coy

Instructions regarding War Diaries and Intelligence Summaries are contained in F. S. Regs., Part II. and the Staff Manual respectively. Title pages will be prepared in manuscript.

Place	Date	Hour	Summary of Events and Information	Remarks and references to Appendices
LAGNICOURT	9-2-18		Enemy artillery displayed considerable activity. During early morning LAGNICOURT was heavily shelled and at intervals from 10am to 6pm the Dumbers road in C22.d and C29.a and Coy HQ at C28.d.99. Sheet 57.c.N.W. was shelled heavily.	
"	10-2-18	1.30am	Enemy fired a number of green lights but no action resulted. LAGNICOURT was shelled intermittently. Relief of Company in accordance with instructions received from 95th Division was commenced. the 193 M.G.Coy taking over positions 5&6.7.8, the section relieved returned to Camp S. FAVREUL.	
"	11-2-18		Remainder of Coy relieved by 193 M.G.Co. as relieved, sections marched to Camp S. FAVREUL.	
FAVREUL	12-2-18		Coy marched to BUCHANAN CAMP, ACHIET LE PETIT. Command of Company taken over by MAJOR R.C.W.BURT.	
BUCHANAN CAMP ACHIET LA PETIT	13-2-18		MAJOR A.P. STRANGE (late O.C) left for UK	
"	14-2-18 – 19-2-18		Formation of machine gun Battalion. Company and Battalion training. Range practice. Inspection.	

From O.C.
  75 Machine Gun Coy

To H.Q.
  75 Brigade

> No. 75 MACHINE GUN COMPANY.
> No. 2093
> Date 1-5-17

Herewith please find original War Diary completed to April 30-17

T. Chunk — Captain,
Commanding
75 MACHINE GUN COY

www.ingramcontent.com/pod-product-compliance
Lightning Source LLC
Chambersburg PA
CBHW081434160426
43193CB00013B/2282